T0133720

CRIMINAL ENTERPRISE INVESTIGATION

CRIMINAL ENTERPRISE INVESTIGATION

THOMAS A. TRIER

CRC Press
Taylor & Francis Group
Boca Raton London New York

CRC Press is an imprint of the
Taylor & Francis Group, an **informa** business

CRC Press
Taylor & Francis Group
6000 Broken Sound Parkway NW, Suite 300
Boca Raton, FL 33487-2742

© 2017 by Taylor & Francis Group, LLC
CRC Press is an imprint of Taylor & Francis Group, an Informa business

No claim to original U.S. Government works

Printed on acid-free paper
Version Date: 20160706

International Standard Book Number-13: 978-1-4987-5944-1 (Hardback)

Library of Congress Cataloging-in-Publication Data

Names: Trier, Thomas A., author.
Title: Criminal enterprise investigation / Thomas A. Trier.
Description: 1 Edition. | Boca Raton : CRC Press, 2017. | Includes bibliographical references and index.
Identifiers: LCCN 2016007072 | ISBN 9781498759441
Subjects: LCSH: Criminal investigation--United States.
Classification: LCC HV8073 .T7295 2016 | DDC 363.250973--dc23
LC record available at https://lccn.loc.gov/2016007072

Visit the Taylor & Francis Web site at
http://www.taylorandfrancis.com

and the CRC Press Web site at
http://www.crcpress.com

Printed and bound in the United States of America by Publishers Graphics,
LLC on sustainably sourced paper.

CONTENTS

SECTION I   Begin

SECTION II *Intelligence*

SECTION III *Investigation*

INTRODUCTION

The reason I wrote this book was to assist law enforcement officers, prosecutors, academics, security professionals, and investigators to understand and develop the principles to dismantle criminal enterprise organizations.

Why is this subject relevant? Why even write a book on how to dismantle criminal enterprises? Who are they? What do they do?

Based on my 28 years of law enforcement experience, I have seen gangs, drug cartels, terrorist cells, and family-based criminal organizations operate with impunity across the spectrum of American communities.

They exist in large metropolitan and rural communities alike. Criminal enterprises are present in many communities, and they usually control the majority of criminal activities in their areas of operation.

You have seen criminal enterprises documented in popular books and movies such as *The Godfather*, *Goodfellas*, and countless other media accounts.

You see real gang shootings and murders on the evening news. Members of criminal enterprises are hidden in communities across the United States.

Whether the criminal enterprise is the Mafia, an Asian Triad, a local gang, or a family of career criminals, they thrive in shadow and anonymity.

Local law enforcement may be aware of the existence of a group of guys committing crimes in their jurisdiction. They arrest them all the time. But they might not realize they are part of an organized crime group. Local cops will arrest members of the criminal enterprise when they break the law. The cops will charge the individuals with the crimes they are committing, say robbery. They may never tie the robberies to a criminal enterprise. That is not to say that local police are not smart or street wise.

Many local cops are sharp. They will figure out their career offenders are part of a criminal enterprise. But they generally lack the resources and expertise to tackle the entire criminal enterprise. They just may not know how to attack the criminal enterprise and dismantle it. Often, they arrest the same people over and over. The police just write it off to career criminals in their jurisdiction, and there isn't much they can do about it.

I believe there is a need for application of the Criminal Enterprise Investigation (CEI) in these situations. The CEI methods call for intelligence-based criminal investigations of entire criminal enterprises.

The CEI path requires tracking the criminal activity in an area and identifying patterns of criminal activity by the same criminal subjects. Through this tracking and analysis, crime problems can be identified and addressed before they become major events.

For example, any law enforcement officer can effect an arrest and obtain a conviction on an individual based upon overwhelming evidence. However, it takes an additional expertise to identify an emerging crime problem to

1. Identify a criminal enterprise operating behind the crime.
2. Initiate a working group to address the criminal enterprise.
3. Disrupt its daily operations.
4. Manage the criminal activity and emerging patterns.

The end game is the dismantlement of the entire criminal enterprise by rooting it out, disabling it from operating, and getting rid of it altogether.

This book will cover the high points of assembling a working group or task force to attack a criminal enterprise.

The CEI process is a little more complicated than working a stand-alone violent crime investigation. In the lone violent crime, the process usually follows the following pattern. The investigator must identify the crime committed. Then they must identify the person who committed the crime and find the motive, opportunity, and method of committing the crime. Then the investigator must gather evidence and compare the evidence to the elements of the crime. The investigator must present the evidence to a prosecutor for charging. The investigator must then assist the prosecutor in proving the crime in a court of law beyond a reasonable doubt.

The CEI process requires each individual crime investigated in the overall case be held to the same standards. However, there are several additional areas required to investigate and dismantle a criminal enterprise. The CEI process usually includes the following additional components:

- Identifying a crime problem
- Identifying the organization
- Identifying personnel
- Identifying leaders, members, and associates
- Identifying an organizational structure

- Proving a criminal enterprise
- Locating and tracking finances

There is also a constant stream of intelligence collected during the course of a CEI. This intelligence must be analyzed, evaluated, and converted to actionable items to assist in the dismantlement of the criminal enterprise. Each of these components will be covered in detail in the chapters of this book.

The CEI investigative strategy outline can be applied by a single agency or investigator. The principle of intelligence-based investigations can be applied to any criminal enterprise. This book will outline key principles and provide past applicable examples that emphasize the investigation of criminal enterprise investigations.

However, it must be pointed out that the CEI is best applied in a working group or task-force environment.

Before tackling a criminal enterprise, there are certain aspects of basic criminal investigation that will be required to address a CEI. Personnel must be proficient at basic investigative skills. Interviewing, report writing, and testifying in court are a few basic skills that a detective, district attorney investigator, or federal agent should have developed before being assigned to complex criminal enterprise investigations.

Ensure that your people are qualified in basic investigative techniques before attempting to tackle a criminal enterprise task force investigation.

Ideally, people who are selected for the task force or working group should be seasoned investigators.

However, I understand this isn't always the case. You may have young inexperienced officers assigned to your investigation, and they may need basic investigative training. In addition, bear in mind that sometimes people get rusty; they may need refresher training. Therefore, I will include a general section on basic investigative techniques along with some opportunities where training may be available to investigators.

CRIME PROBLEM

One of the main themes of this book will be evaluating a crime problem. The term "crime problem" can be best described as a spike in violent crimes, such as car jackings, robberies, and muggings, that gets noticed by the public. And this increase in criminal activity is within and/or across several law enforcement jurisdictions.

One of the preliminary steps in addressing a crime problem is conducting an initial assessment. Another step is determining who will be investigating the criminal enterprise identified.

It may take additional assessment and evaluation to determine if there is a criminal enterprise involved. The initial assessment of the crime problem may be conducted by one or two investigators from the same or more than one jurisdiction.

Forming and formalizing a task force take time, effort, and a true mission focus on an assessed and identified crime problem. The initial assessment may be also conducted by analysts, but the enterprise theory of investigation will require investigators to gather evidence and track criminals, informants, and finances, in fact all aspects of the targeted criminal enterprise to be successful.

As the crime problem is identified, the initial assessment should also include a section on jurisdiction to evaluate what resources may be called upon to assist or participate in the overall investigation. Another priority of the assessment will be identifying a group responsible and their patterns of activity.

To address the initial assessment of a crime problem, an informal working group should be considered. This group may consist of various agencies and personnel that may have an interest in the crime problem and may initially consist of weekly meetings to compare information. The working group may be the foundation of a formal task force in the future, but it may also be sufficient to solve the crime problem it was formed to address.

Once the initial assessment of the criminal problem has identified a criminal enterprise involved, investigators should begin analyzing the criminal enterprise, determining its patterns of criminal activity, past and present arrests, convictions, and prosecutions.

Begin by identifying the people involved with the criminal enterprise including, but not limited to, their leadership, general membership, associates, enemies, family members, and past investigative agencies that may have investigated the enterprise.

What are the enterprise vulnerabilities? What methods of financing are they utilizing? Do they have legitimate jobs, businesses, or income?

Also, be aware that working group and/or task force agency participation will fluctuate during the course of an investigation. A side note for the initial assessment is the political environment of the law enforcement departments within the jurisdiction where the criminal enterprise exists. We will touch on the politics of law enforcement agencies and the impact of politics on major investigations.

The politics of a law enforcement agency may greatly affect the investigative efforts of the working group. For example, a problem ensues if a county sheriff's office denies there is a gang problem in the county and if through the course of investigation the working group, which includes a deputy, identifies a gang responsible for a series of murders, robberies, and significant drug trafficking activity.

The sheriff who denied the problem in the first place is put in a bad position. Since he or she is an elected official, he or she has to admit either he or she has a gang problem or that these crimes were committed on his or her watch, under his or her nose. If so, he or she takes a chance that in the next election his or her opponent will attack him or her unless he or she can emphasize the efforts of the working group to address the crime problem. His or her other choice is to continue to deny the gang problem and pull the deputy from the working group and leave the investigation. So you see how politics can greatly affect the investigative efforts of a working group or task force.

Another area and probably the most important to consider when investigating a criminal enterprise is prosecution. Without effective prosecution, a thorough well-investigated case might yield a gold mine of intelligence. But without effective prosecutive action, the goal, the mission to disrupt and dismantle the criminal enterprise responsible for the crime problem, will not be met.

The success of the CEI depends on effective prosecution at the local, state, and federal levels throughout the course of the investigation. The early involvement of prosecuting attorneys at all these levels is imperative for success.

Early involvement of prosecutors is a benefit to investigators that cannot be overemphasized. The goal is to involve the prosecutors and assimilate them to the level they start calling the investigation "my case." Once the prosecutors are invested in the investigation to the level they have personal ownership, they will give investigators their undivided attention and the best they have to offer. Engagement for prosecutors is essential for successful prosecutions.

There is nothing more rewarding than being a contributing member of a task force that investigates and meets the goal of the disruption and dismantlement of a criminal enterprise that once operated with autonomy across several jurisdictions. The positive relationships built between law enforcement officials and prosecutors who spend endless hours together preparing search and arrest warrant affidavits, grand jury testimony, and the preparation for trials have lifelong rewards.

I have also successfully applied the intelligence-based investigative techniques to the counterterrorism arena and private sector security. The application in these areas is also documented in more detail in Chapters 25 and 26.

A couple of quick disclaimers:

Some of the names of people on both sides of this investigation, law enforcement, and criminal have been substituted with pseudonyms.

Any opinions in this book are mine and not those of the Federal Bureau of Investigation.

ABOUT THE AUTHOR

Thomas A. Trier served as a special agent of the Federal Bureau of Investigation (FBI) for 25 years, including 13 years in the FBI management program. He attained the rank of the assistant special agent in charge in the Intelligence Branch of the FBI Washington Field Office. His fields of expertise are investigating criminal and terrorist enterprises, including extensive service overseas and development of intelligence programs.

Trier served two and a half years as the leader of Corporate Security for a midwestern electrical-transmission-only utility company. He was accountable for managing security projects and processes across the company to enhance overall security and reduce Corporate Security risk. He developed a security intelligence program that defined and analyzed internal, external, and electrical industry threats to the enterprise and formed collaborative working groups to reduce risk through a well-developed security plan.

He provides advisory services through Security Intelligence Consulting LLC, Milwaukee, WI.

Section I

Begin

1

Criminal Enterprise Investigations
Background

In order to help explain my understanding in conducting criminal enterprise investigations, I will provide some of my background and experiences. This is important to demonstrate my personal development and experience regarding criminal enterprise investigations.

I spent 25 years as a special agent of the Federal Bureau of Investigation (FBI); the dates are important because of the major events that happened during my FBI service from 1986 to 2011.

I was assigned to the Seattle Office after completion of the 17-week training at the FBI New Agents Academy in Quantico, Virginia. I was assigned to the Violent Crimes Squad and investigated a variety of violent crimes, bank robberies, extortions, kidnapping cases, bombings, and domestic terrorism.

At the time, the small-to-medium offices of the FBI contained only new agents and the most senior of agents who had enough seniority to obtain the "office of preference" transfer, which meant they were close to retirement. At the time, agents were required to retire at age 55; in 1990, was raised the mandatory retirement age to 57.

This is important because the core of FBI agents with 5–20 years of experience were in the "top twelve" offices, which were the biggest offices in the country, including New York, Los Angeles, and San Francisco. New agents were transferred to these offices after acquiring five years of experience in a small or medium office.

I was no exception and in January of 1991, I was transferred from Seattle to the Los Angeles Office. At the time, Los Angeles was the bank robbery capitol of the United States, with more than 2800 bank robberies a year. I was assigned to work bank robberies in the West Covina Resident Agency (a satellite office of the Los Angeles Division), which averaged about 400 bank robberies a year.

Drugs such as cocaine and heroin were a major reason for the bank robbery problems during that time. Addicts would fuel their habits through a series of bank robberies sometimes committing more than 20 bank robberies before they were caught. We spent our time trying to identify these serial bank robbers and charge them with enough robberies to keep them off the streets. Besides drug addicts, we also noticed a large number of African-American adolescents were robbing banks, in violent and spectacular ways.

Eventually, by using the intelligence-based techniques detailed in this book, we identified a trend with the young African-Americans. Rollin 60s gang leaders used bank robberies as an initiation criterion for young men who wanted to join their gang. The gang leaders would supply these young men with firearms and tell them to rob banks and give them the money. The inexperienced robbers would commit rookie mistakes. They would shoot up the banks, strike tellers, and stay in the banks too long. The police would then show and up often as not, the robbers were shot and sometimes killed.

These robbery investigations were some of the earliest experiences I had with the utilization of intelligence, paralleling the FBI's traditional investigative techniques. Concentrating investigation and prosecution on the gang leaders behind the robbery initiations contributed to the reduction of bank robberies in Los Angeles in the 1990s. Of course, it wasn't the only factor, as banks concentrated their assets and bought each other out, they closed many branches, added extra security, and trained their personnel regarding bank robberies. These steps contributed to the reduction of bank robberies.

In 1994, I was reassigned from bank robberies to investigate Mexican Drug Trafficking Organizations (MDTOs). This was significant, as it was my first opportunity to formally investigate criminal enterprises.

The FBI required a link to an international group to open a drug case, and FBI Headquarters (FBIHQ) did not want to expend their resources on local street drug dealers. Therefore, you had to develop hard ties to MDTOs such as the Arellano-Félix Organization or the Joaquin Guzman Organization. This required street agents to coordinate with local law enforcement and develop intelligence regarding the targeted group prior to opening a formal investigation. These investigations also were coordinated with the Drug Enforcement Agency (DEA), as they were the primary agency regarding narcotics investigations; no one wanted to get into a "blue on blue" (cop vs. cop) situation. The FBI was no different and did not want to be buying 25 kilograms of cocaine from the DEA, or become involved in an armed confrontation with other cops.

The intelligence gathering and criminal analysis of the MDTO investigations that I learned in the early 1990s was based on the intelligence-based criminal investigation activities that I utilized in working gangs in the late 1990s. I would also use these techniques in Iraq in 2007 while investigating terrorist cells.

The basic premise is finding out whom we are targeting; finding their true backgrounds, defining their capabilities, connections, enemies, family members, and weaknesses and vulnerabilities were categories that didn't change from enterprise to enterprise. The major difference between terrorist and criminal investigations was the element of intent; in the criminal world, intent always implied that the criminal was breaking the law, and intent was easy to prove. However, it was a little harder to prove in some of the terrorist or private sector investigations that I conducted.

By 1999, I began working gang investigations in Los Angeles area, specifically the Nazi Lowriders (NLR), which was a white supremacist gang with ties to the Aryan Brotherhood. By then, I had become very familiar with the basic principles of the criminal enterprise theory of investigation, and readily applied them to this group.

At the time, the NLR totaled about 1500 members in California and Nevada. The first order of business was to form a task force; the Ontario Police Department had five persons working with the DEA, as the NLR was manufacturing and distributing crystal methamphetamine in major cities in California to finance their operations in and out of the California Department of Corrections (CDC) facilities.

However, the amounts of meth they were dealing were nowhere near the amounts being brought up from Mexico from the MDTOs, so DEA relinquished the case to the FBI.

The CDC had a special services unit (SSU) that assigned a person to the task force, so did the Fontana and Upland Police Departments along with the Alcohol Tobacco and Firearms, which lent an agent part time on an as-needed basis. The U.S. Attorney's Office had already assigned an extremely effective assistant U.S. attorney to the case. The FBI gave me two newer agents, and the NLR Task Force was formed with over a dozen of law enforcement officers with the mission of the disruption and dismantlement of the NLR as an effective criminal enterprise.

With the task force officially formed, the next steps were the identification of the leaders of the NLR, who was making things happen and as with the MDTOs years earlier. Priorities included finding out who we were targeting, finding their true backgrounds, defining their capabilities, connections, enemies, family members, and weaknesses and vulnerabilities.

In the course of the investigation, I had to demonstrate some leadership; the assigned police officers wanted to concentrate all the task force efforts on making new cases, and I (as well as the U.S. attorney) wanted to also collect and review historical cases related to the 16 NLR leaders to utilize Racketeer Influenced and Corrupt Organizations charges on the leadership, so I proposed a compromise. Two days a week, the entire task force would review assigned cases under my supervision, and three days a week, we would pursue new cases the police were investigating on NLR members.

The main focus of the investigation would concentrate on the leaders of the NLR, but the street-level enforcement would continue, which we called "hooking and booking." It was a good practice and a specific deterrent, knocking down NLR members' meth houses and putting them in jail on local or state charges. It was a lot of hustling, but it supplied us with an extremely valuable and strategic resource; call them informants, sources, rats, or whatever, the information gleaned from NLR insiders was invaluable.

Our overall efforts ensured that we knew what the NLR was doing before they were doing it. It was the best example of intelligence gathering, analysis, and application that I had experienced up to that time.

The intelligence network we built included every law enforcement agency with a footprint in California: a network of more than 30 working informants, analysis from the Joint Drug Intelligence Group (JDIG), and an operational arm of 12 officers/agents.

In August 2001, I took a promotion to supervisory special agent in the Safe Streets and Gang Unit (SSGU) at the FBIHQ. The SSGU was responsible for administrative oversight of all FBI gang investigations across the United States. It was also responsible for developing and implementing strategy to target the most dangerous and organized gangs with the potential to become a national threat.

The intelligence lessons learned in Los Angeles were reinforced while at FBIHQ, reading, evaluating, and analyzing all the gang intelligence that poured into FBIHQ; the mission to determine the gangs with potential national impact was invaluable to me. My experience at FBIHQ gave me a strategic view and developed my strategic long-term planning skills. Then the terrorist attacks happened on November 9, 2001 while I was at FBIHQ. Needless to say, this event greatly impacted all FBI missions.

The lessons I learned as an FBI Agent, by applying criminal intelligence through the criminal enterprise theory of investigation, progressed from investigating bank robberies to drug trafficking organizations and gangs in Los Angeles, and as an supervisory special agent in the SSGU at FBIHQ were the basis for the tests that were to come. Eventually, I found myself applying these techniques to terrorist groups in Iraq in 2007.

In 2008, I took another promotion and became an intelligence assistant special agent in charge (ASAC) of the Washington Field Office (WFO) in Washington DC. The time that I spent as the intelligence ASAC in WFO truly solidified my skills.

Through years of investigative experience, I have developed a certain mindset. For me, any problem includes an intelligence overview and critical thinking through comprehensive analysis, evaluation, and action on collected data.

My intentions of writing this book were to document lessons learned, including the pitfalls, in investigating a criminal enterprise. Unfortunately for me, I learned a lot of things through the "school of hard knocks," meaning that I learned by doing. Sometimes, the lessons were hard ones, and I wished that I could go back and apply what I had learned to be more effective (Table 1.1).

So, taking what I had learned, I am attempting to author a product that I could give to young Special Agent Thomas A. Trier coming out of the FBI Academy in 1986. A guide that illustrates examples and helps him

Table 1.1 Task Force Participation Chart

Year	Task Force	Mission	Role
1992	West Covina bank robbery Task Force	Bank robberies	Task force coordinator
1994	West Covina drug Task Force	Drug investigations	Task force coordinator
1995	West Covina White-Collar Mortgage Fraud Task Force	Mortgage fraud investigations	Task force coordinator
1999	Nazi Lowrider Task Force	Gang investigations	Task force coordinator
2001	Watchlist Resolution Team	Counterterrorism	Participant
2001	Safe Streets and Gang Unit	Gang investigations	FBI supervisor
2003	Madison Joint Terrorism Task Force	Counterterrorism	FBI supervisor
2005	Rock County Gang Task Force	Gang investigations	FBI supervisor
2008	Iraq Task Forces (five)	Counterterrorism and criminal	FBI deputy commander
2009	Washington Field Office Intelligence Working Groups	Counterterrorism, counterintelligence, and criminal	Assistant special agent in charge
2010	Madison Mortgage Fraud Task Force	Mortgage fraud	Task force coordinator

understand available avenues to conduct a complex investigation into a criminal enterprise.

Knowing the young cocky agent he was, he probably won't read it until 1994, when he starts working drugs in Los Angeles. But I want to make it available to those who may want to read it and learn from my success and failures.

2

Identify the Crime Problem

With any law enforcement organization, whether local, state, federal, investigative, or prosecutive, there is no lack of opportunity for those who want to work. For those who are truly involved in their profession and believe in doing the right thing, that is, "defending the Constitution and protecting the weak," there are endless opportunities.

This book is for those who want to do the right thing, the hardworking officers, agents, and prosecutors who want to identify and address crime problems in their jurisdictions because if they don't, no one else will, and the criminals will win.

My goal is to write a book that I would have liked to have 30 years ago when I first hit the streets as a new FBI agent. How do I investigate an enterprise? What do I do and how do I do it? Where are the pitfalls? Problems? How do I address these hurdles when I come across them? How do I get a task force together?

So far I have used the words, "crime problem," to identify an area of criminal activity that may be present in or across several jurisdictions. So what am I talking about? It could be any kind of criminal activity that comes to the attention of the public and/or civic leaders and that requires interdiction by law enforcement.

Examples could include but are not limited to spikes in the following criminal activity: robberies, car jackings, burglaries, drug trafficking, prostitution, bribery, counterfeiting, theft, embezzlement, fraud, dealing in obscene matter, obstruction of justice, slavery, racketeering, gambling, money laundering, and commission of murder-for-hire. The criminal activity could just about include anything that is illegal. The key to identifying a crime problem is the identifiable criminal activity wasn't there in the past but has become prevalent and has been affecting the public.

Please make no mistake. I know as well as you do that as long as there are people, there will be criminal activity. People will shoot, rob, and kill each other. It is part of life. However, when a criminal activity spikes and remains as a disturbing constant, there is usually an underlying element behind the scenes. That is where you will find your criminal enterprise.

In Chapter 1, we discussed several crime problems that I personally investigated: bank robberies, drug trafficking, and gang problems in Los Angeles. There have been other crime problems that I investigated and applied these techniques such as a slave trafficking ring in Seattle, Washington; a serial killer in Seattle; a kidnapping ring in Los Angeles, California; gangs in Wisconsin, and a serial rapist in Madison, Wisconsin, to name a few.

If civic leaders or pressure from the community comes to law enforcement and suggests they address a crime problem, there is bound to be some initial intelligence on what constitutes the perceived crime problem. They should have some idea of what is going on in the community. This will develop leads for law enforcement to follow.

Even if the initial law enforcement working group only consists of two people, the gathering, evaluation, analysis, and assessment of the crime problem are essential. Ensure that the assessment is documented and available for presentation to potential task force member organization, supervisors, prosecutors, and appropriate headquarters elements. Once written, parts of the initial assessment will come into play throughout the investigation.

Start the assessment with basic investigation 101 (see Figures 2.1 and 2.2). Identify who is responsible for the criminal activity. If you know the individuals who commit the crimes, check if there is a group behind them? What is their pattern of criminal activity? Once you identify who is behind the crime problem, and the criminal activity they are committing, building the cases against them should be second nature to an experienced investigator.

Sometimes, the criminal activity conceals itself to the underbelly of society. When the criminal activity crosses over into the mainstream and affects the general population, it is often described as an "epidemic."

As stated earlier, document the findings in the assessment and prepare to brief appropriate personnel on your findings. In addition, continue to assess and document the gist of the crime problem, and how you are addressing it throughout the entire life cycle of the investigation.

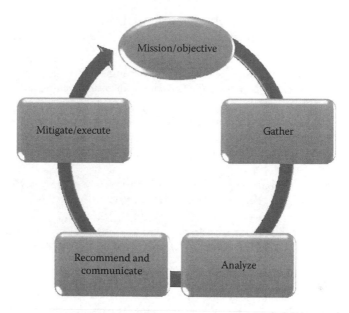

Figure 2.1 Analysis chart.

Effective communication is one of the critical keys to success in any program and should be part of every component of your crime problem analysis. The following touches on some key points for effective communication.

From the initial assessment of your crime problem to the final phases of the implementation of your tactical plans, all affected parties should be informed and should be aware of the assessment and its impact on their operations. If possible, goals, objectives, operations, procedures, and mission statements should be effectively communicated to working group partners and future task force members.

Ensure that executives from your agency are involved and engaged early on in the process. This can be done through concise presentations using PowerPoint templates, explaining the benefits of the working group through the prevention of crimes by targeting and dismantling the targeted criminal enterprise. Drafted action plans (basic five-paragraph operations orders) can also play an important role in briefing future task force and your own executives (see box "Action Plan").

Many of the examples in this book will describe actions we took to investigate the Nazi Lowriders (NLR) in Los Angeles. Let's move

ANALYSIS METHODOLOGY

The following methodology can be used to conduct the initial assessment of the crime problem:

1) Collect, evaluate, and analyze existing documents regarding the crime problem. Police reports, newspaper articles, and court documents are all examples of intelligence.

2) Check with area law enforcement to determine if anyone is currently investigating the crime problem.

3) Check to determine if there have been past investigations. Gather any past intelligence for analysis.

4) Explore jurisdictional responsibilities within the crime problem. Who should be involved? Feds? State? Local law enforcement? Other non-law enforcement?

5) Explore the formation of a working group with agencies that investigated the crime problem in the past or are currently investigating the crime problem.

6) Identify subjects responsible for the crime problem.

7) Start an organizational chart listing subjects, members, and associates.

8) Define criminal activity. What laws are being broken? At what level? Federal? State? Local?

9) Document results of initial assessment of the crime problem.

10) Document recommendations to address the crime problem.

11) Prepare PowerPoint briefing presentation of the initial assessment of the crime problem and recommendations for resolution and present to potential task force executives.

Figure 2.2 Analysis methodology.

on to Chapter 3, and I will tell you how we investigated the NLR in Los Angeles.

NLR was a violent prison gang, formed by white inmates, to control the white prison population. The NLR was originally formed in the California Penal system and spread across the entire United States.

As the organization developed, a white supremacist philosophy was adopted. Status in the gang was obtained by violent acts carried out by its members. Members of the NLR leadership aspired to the Aryan Brotherhood membership in exchange for loyalty and the commission of violent acts committed for the Aryan Brotherhood.

The NLR also controlled much of the drug trafficking conducted by white inmates in the penal system. The NLR demanded one-third of all

ACTION PLAN

An action plan is based upon the five-paragraph operation order utilized by the U.S. Army. It is extremely helpful to set the focus for a team and ensure everyone understands their roles in the mission. The five paragraphs are situation, mission, execution, administrative, and command and control. Each paragraph has a purpose. The following can be used as a guide of what to write in each paragraph. As an example, I have also included an action plan that I wrote to address the copper theft problem at the electrical utility company.

Situation: Describe the problem that will be addressed by the action plan. Be concise.

Mission: Describe what you expect to accomplish through the action plan. What is the overall mission of the team that is addressing the problem summarized in the *Situation* paragraph? One or two sentences will suffice.

Execution: This is usually the lengthiest paragraph of the action plan. Here, you will detail specific assignments to teams and individuals on those teams, the more specific the details the better.

Administrative: Describe equipment needs. Describe deadlines, timelines, and a measure of progress.

Command and control: Describe who is in charge and the roles of key personnel.

drugs brought into the prison system by white inmates. Upon receiving narcotics, the NLR then provided protection from Mexican and African-American inmates, to the white drug traffickers. The NLR committed numerous violent acts, including murder, attempted murder, assault, robbery, and extortion in furtherance of their organization. The victims of these violent acts were usually other white inmates who did not follow the rules set by the NLR.

When we started the NLR Task Force, there were over 1500 NLR members and associates in the western United States. They were all criminals, and the number of crimes they were committing was astronomical. Needless to say, it was a daunting task to investigate the NLR as a criminal enterprise. One person would have a difficult time addressing such a crime problem. We needed a task force to take on the NLR.

3

Build Law Enforcement Working Group

Any task force is a mix of jurisdictions and roles, although there is no magic bullet that would fit into a task force matrix. The following is a suggestion to some potential members that could be added in forming a task force, provided there is a need for their specific expertise. See Table 3.1 for agency roles and responsibilities in a task force.

Still, life is far from ideal, and investigations and task forces often take on a life of their own. I will use the example of the Los Angeles FBI Nazi Lowriders (NLR) Task Force throughout this book to demonstrate what we personally encountered in the course of our investigation into the NLR.

Sometimes, the crime problem comes to light in unexpected and unusual ways. They say life is stranger than fiction, and the start of the NLR Task Force in Los Angeles was a combination of several factors, some strange and others logical. On the logical side, in or around 1998, the San Bernardino Sheriff's Office had been gathering intelligence on the NLR through a series of crimes that had occurred in their jurisdiction.

The initial analysis conducted by the California Department of Corrections (CDC) and the San Bernardino Sheriff's Office defined the NLR. Let me summarize their findings.

The NLR was first formed within the California Penal system during the 1970s. In the 1990s, the NLR had an estimated membership of over 1500 members. It was a prison gang that comprised white males who espoused white supremacist philosophy and committed criminal acts to

15

Table 3.1 Agency Roles and Responsibilities Matrix

Agency	Jurisdiction	Role/Responsibility
FBI	Federal	Investigation of over 300 federal violations across the spectrum
DEA	Federal	Investigation of drug violations
ATF	Federal	Investigation of gun violations and gang work
ICE	Federal	Investigation of immigration violations
U.S. Postal Service	Federal	Investigations involving the U.S. Mail
State Police	State	Investigations at the state level
Highway Patrol	State	Responsible for state highway enforcement
Parole	State	State parole responsibility
Probation	State/local	State and local probation responsibility
Local Police	Local	Local law enforcement generic to their city, county, or defined jurisdiction

benefit the organization. NLR members had committed multiple criminal acts to further the NLR as an organization. They committed hate crimes against minorities to further their own beliefs of white racial purity in American society.

NLR members and their associates migrated into the general public when they were released from prison. In 1998, San Bernardino Sheriff's Department estimated that between 1000 and 1500 NLR members were in California state prisons. They also estimated 200–400 NLR members operating freely on the streets in San Bernardino County.

A review of crime reports involving NLR members showed that their criminal activity included murder, attempted murder, assault with a deadly weapon, and numerous drug violations. The drug violations included many types of illegal narcotics, but analysis indicated that the NLR favored the manufacture and distribution of methamphetamine.

The NLR set up proprietorship of geographical areas and claimed ownership of all drug dealing activities in those areas. They would use violence and intimidation to collect "taxes" from other methamphetamine producers in the area they claimed.

Investigation also revealed that the NLR gang members committed hate crimes as a result of their white supremacist philosophy. The gang was closely associated with the Aryan Brotherhood (AB). Many NLR leaders aspired to attain AB membership and committed criminal acts at the behest of the AB leadership.

In the late 1990s, the San Bernardino Sheriff's Office Intelligence Unit and CDC expanded their analysis to include NLR activities throughout California. What they discovered was that the NLR was an expansive, structured, and an organized enterprise. They contacted the U.S. Attorney's Office in Los Angeles. They coordinated their efforts with Assistant U.S. Attorney (AUSA) Charlene Olmedo, who was interested in their findings.

Around the same time, and this is the strange part, the Ontario Police Department busted a methamphetamine laboratory in a house next to the home of a local politician in Ontario, California. The meth lab was tied to the NLR and the politician told the chief of police to investigate the NLR. The Ontario Police Department dedicated a police sergeant and four officers to work on the NLR. The Ontario Police Department engaged the FBI in Riverside, California, to work with them.

The FBI assigned an agent and formalized the NLR Task Force by initiating a Safe Streets and Gang Task Force through the Safe Streets and Gang Unit at FBI Headquarters. The formalization of the task force allowed the FBI to pay for overtime and supply equipment to police officers on the task force. The initial task force also included the CDC Special Services Unit (SSU), the Upland Police Department, and the Fontana Police Department.

Eventually, two NLR Task Forces (Ontario and San Bernardino) merged under the umbrella of the FBI-led Safe Street Task Force. AUSA Olmedo joined the FBI NLR Task Force; however, the San Bernardino Sheriff's Office did not formally participate in the FBI NLR Task Force. They allowed one of their deputies knowledgeable about the NLR work behind the scenes but would not formally commit to the task force. I found out why much later. We will discuss the underlying reasons later in Chapter 4.

So by the end of 1998, the NLR Task Force was an AUSA; FBI agent; SSU; and Fontana, Upland, and Ontario Police Departments. However, within a year, there was trouble in paradise. The Ontario Police Department believed the FBI was moving too slow in their investigative efforts. In all fairness, the FBI agent initially assigned to lead the NLR investigation was young and inexperienced. He just didn't know how to investigate a major case.

So, in a twist and distraction, the Ontario Police Department disengaged themselves from the formal FBI task force. They went to the Drug Enforcement Agency (DEA) looking for better service in the NLR investigation. The AUSA, SSU, and Fontana and Upland Police Departments followed the Ontario Police Department lead and went with them to the DEA. The FBI agent assigned to the NLR Task Force continued to work with the task force but in a secondary role.

Soon, the problems mounted for the new DEA NLR Task Force. Although the NLR was manufacturing and distributing methamphetamine in California, NLR production was limited to distributing ounces. The Mexican cartels were distributing methamphetamine in pounds and throughout the entire United States. So, the NLR was deemed a lower priority for the DEA than it had been for the FBI.

The DEA could not deliver on the Ontario Police Department's high expectations for the NLR investigation. Nevertheless, the NLR was committing violent acts, and that was of great interest to the FBI.

During this period, I was reassigned to the Riverside, California, Resident Agency of the Los Angeles Division of the FBI. I had never heard of the NLR and was not assigned to the NLR Task Force.

By 1999, I had 13 years of experience investigating cases. My investigative background included investigation of major violent crimes such as bank robbery and kidnapping rings, along with criminal enterprises, specifically, Mexican Drug Trafficking Organizations (MDTOs).

My initial assignment in Riverside was to work on the existing Fugitive Task Force. To make a long story short, one of the fugitives I started chasing was also an NLR subject that the Ontario Police Department wanted for murder. We eventually pooled resources of with the NLR Task Force. Together, we ultimately caught the subject, after a car chase and foot pursuit.

Success breeds success. The FBI eventually resumed the lead role in the NLR Task Force. I assumed the role as lead case agent. I had two other younger agents assigned to work with me. The Ontario and Fontana Police Departments and SSU rejoined the NLR Task Force along with AUSA Olmedo. Ancillary members included the San Bernardino County Sheriff's Office, the DEA, the Bureau of Alcohol, Tobacco, Firearms and Explosives (ATF), the Postal Service, the Internal Revenue Service, and the San Bernardino County District Attorney's Office.

Once re-formed and with the NLR Task Force under FBI leadership, I ensured that the NLR Task Force concentrated their efforts on a clearly defined investigative game plan. To provide focus to the task force, we developed a clear set mission. The mission to "disrupt and dismantle the NLR through investigation and effective prosecution" was adopted.

The U.S. Attorney's Office pursued Racketeer Influenced and Corrupt Organizations (RICO) charges against the NLR leadership. A federal grand jury (FGJ) was convened in the year 2000. The FGJ heard the testimony of witnesses to Violent Crimes in Aid of Racketeering and RICO in reference to gangs. The FGJ also heard general testimony of NLR members that were used to testify against NLR leadership. Witnesses classified as NLR and gang experts from law enforcement also testified to the FGJ.

In order to accomplish the overall defined mission, the task force adopted a two-pronged submission approach to the NLR investigation.

The disruption mission was to target any and all NLR members and their associates and business connections with any and all charges possible. The disruption phase was initiated to disrupt the daily operations of the NLR. For example, if an NLR member was getting out of prison on parole and information was received that he was involved in drug charges, we would pursue all avenues to disrupt his activities. The more NLR members we caught red-handed, the more potential witnesses we had against the leaders.

The dismantlement mission was to identify the leaders of the NLR and utilize the RICO statutes to address their murderous activities.

The two-pronged approach proved very effective in the NLR case. The disruption phase allowed the local police the opportunity to enforce street crimes in their jurisdiction. This allowed their executives to see quick and sustained results. The dismantlement phase accomplished the overall mission and allowed the FBI to exercise the RICO investigation. By the time we finished the investigation, we were a close-knit team. The experience was personally rewarding to each member of the NLR Task Force.

However, as explained, the road to the formalization and effective operations in the NLR Task Force was not clear cut or defined. As you form your own task force or working group, be prepared to navigate through adversity. Some of the adversity will be described in Chapter 4.

4

Politics

In this chapter, we will touch on politics, that is, law enforcement agency politics and their potential impact on investigations.

There is no doubt that one of the most rewarding and most difficult accomplishments that a law enforcement official can claim is the initiation of an effective and efficient task force, and then to focus its efforts to successfully address a significant crime problem.

The rewards to individual task force members include the small unit camaraderie and *esprit de corps* that develops between task force members. These relationships solidify as they concentrate their efforts on the single goal of disrupting and dismantling a criminal enterprise. Over time, task force members will become loyal to each other and form a bond that overcomes initial apprehension and or agency animosity.

To dismantle a criminal organization, which in the recent past seemed to be above the law and untouchable, is the pinnacle of law enforcement prowess.

The leader of the task force must ensure that the members engage in the mission of the task force and concentrate their efforts on the targeted criminal enterprise. If a task force member will not engage in the task force mission, if they insist on personal or departmental objectives, replace them as soon as you can. The cohesion of the task force will be threatened by one individual operating in a vacuum.

At the federal level, the political difficulty often comes in the interagency rivalry that exists among the federal agencies with jurisdiction. As in the example with the NLR, the FBI, DEA, and ATF all had investigative interest and jurisdiction in the NLR—the FBI because of the gang activity, the DEA because of the drug activity, and the ATF because of the firearms violations. In the NLR investigation, there was no initial squabbling as the FBI ran independent.

Nonetheless, as stated earlier, the local departments left the FBI task force and went to the DEA with the NLR case. Eventually, the DEA did not believe the volume of drugs was a high priority for them, and the locals went back to the FBI task force. Had there been a proper prior coordination between the FBI and DEA regarding the shared intelligence on the volume of drugs, the NLR was manufacturing and distributing may have saved everyone a lot of time.

After the terrorist attacks on September 11, 2001, the ATF became heavily involved in gang investigations. With the majority of FBI resources concentrated on the terrorist cases, the FBI gang resources were diminished. The ATF is currently a major player in gang cases.

During the time of the NLR investigation (late 1990s), the ATF's role was to assist with firearm charges. The bottom line is if you are going to initiate an investigation into a crime problem that crosses jurisdictions across federal agencies, contact those agencies and conduct some initial de-confliction. Talk to them and determine if they are already investigating the enterprise that you are targeting. Offer to work with them if they are investigating the targeted group. If they aren't investigating the criminal enterprise and do not want to participate, do yourself a favor and take time to document the conversation in an official memorandum.

The documentation of these meetings is a critical piece of advice. If the investigation starts to take off and becomes successful, the same agency that refused to participate initially may raise hell and accuse you of not coordinating. The memo documenting the initial contact could come in very handy in the future. Live by the golden rule and treat others like how you want to be treated, but also shield yourself with effective and concise documentation. Remember, "If it isn't written down, it doesn't exist."

Let's move on to state agencies as potential task force members. Unlike the federal brothers and sisters that may have parallel or the same jurisdiction, most state agencies have different jurisdictions, statutes, and charges from their federal counterparts.

Simply stated, the state agencies can and will bring additional investigative tools to the same crime problem without the interagency competition that may exist between two federal agencies.

The problem with the state derives from the competition for resources by federal agencies who are addressing a myriad of crime problems across a state's territory. The state agency must prioritize crime problems and allocate limited resources. Always be aware and realistic as to where your crime problem rates regarding the state agency's priorities. If your crime problem is high on their priority list, solicit them for assistance. If it is not high on their priority list, brief them on the crime problem and document the conversation. If they do not join the task force initially, as their priorities change and evolve, the state agency may join the task force in the future.

Next, let's discuss the local county sheriff's office. Since most county sheriffs are elected, this is a unique contact and calls for extra finesse. Because they are up for election approximately every four years, they are reluctant to take on a crime problem that makes it look like they were either asleep at the switch or bungling their responsibility.

This can be explained easily enough. Suppose that a sheriff in office has been saying there is no gang problem in his territory for the past three years. As a young federal agent, you bring a proposal to join a task force that is investigating a gang that has killed 10 people in his county in the past four years. Your initial proposal may contradict everything that he has been saying. You may even be contradicting the political platform the sheriff has started for his re-election. Based on these circumstances, do not expect the sheriff to join your formalized task force. The best you can hope for is support from street deputies on raids when you operate in their county. Be aware of the current situation and apply appropriate (be ethical) political finesse in these matters. Know where you stand and be realistic in your expectations.

Major metropolitan police departments have a special niche in federally formed task forces. Many of the large departments, say over 1000 sworn officers, do not believe that federal agencies have anything to contribute to their department's mission. Many of them believe they have similar or even better resources than the federal agencies.

Especially in this modern age, the Internet, e-mail, and electronic communications between large municipal police departments have diminished the need for coordination with the FBI in criminal matters. Why call the FBI for a fugitive lead in Texas? The New York Police Department can e-mail a lead on a fugitive to the Dallas Police Department, who will pick them up without any problem. Why bother with the FBI?

Any and all of these political problems can be overcome by developing substantial and meaningful personable relationships with any of the agencies within your jurisdiction.

For example, I had a hell of a time in Los Angeles in the early 1990s. I had been reassigned to working drug investigations from working bank robberies, which I had done for years.

I teamed up with a local medium-sized police department who had identified a drug trafficking ring in their territory. The ring was a branch of a major drug trafficking ring out of Tijuana, Mexico. The local police had compiled a wealth of information and intelligence on the criminal enterprise. I took the police department intelligence binders to study.

In the meantime, I was instructed to coordinate with the DEA by my FBI supervisor. When I investigated the bank robberies, I shared every piece of intelligence with other investigative law enforcement agencies. I didn't see a problem with sharing everything we had with the DEA on this MDTO.

So, when the lead detective and I met with the DEA, I provided the intelligence books to them in good faith. They took the books, copied them. Then told me they had been investigating the group for a while. We were to "back off."

The next day, the DEA "door knocked" two of the locations in the books and seized 225 kilograms of cocaine and arrested three people. They didn't call us to accompany them.

The detective that I was working with told me I was a "dumb ass." I realized that I needed to change my tactics from what I had learned by working bank robberies. Just sharing information wasn't what they did in the drug game in Los Angeles in the 1990s.

Although I agreed with the detective that I was a "dumb ass," I believed my strategy was sound in developing good solid contacts across all law enforcement agencies. I just had to do it at the right time. I had to learn to develop the appropriate situational awareness to adjust to the political climate of major law enforcement politics.

I devoted a couple of weeks talking to other FBI agents that were working drug cases and developed a list of DEA agents they worked with and trusted.

From the information I received from the other FBI agents, I found a DEA agent that worked in my territory and opened a dialogue. We developed a relationship. We worked well together, to the point that we shared case information without screwing each other over. The DEA agent became my personal friend and someone I could trust in an agency that constantly feuded with my agency. The theme is to develop the personal contacts and depend on trusted associates to get the job done.

Personal relationships will overcome adversity when investigating cases and forming working relationships. Ensure that you maintain and practice high standards. Don't lie or cheat in dealing with other agencies. Stay professional and you will develop a reputation as a standup guy/gal.

As a final note on politics, every U.S. Attorney's Office takes orders from the U.S. attorney general in Washington DC. Every new administration that assumes control of the White House appoints its own U.S. attorney general. The new president also replaces each U.S. attorney across all judicial districts. This is done according to party lines. National politics can play a huge role on which cases are prosecuted across the country.

For example, the Obama administration believed that most people incarcerated for "nonviolent" drug offenses under minimum maximum sentences were "victims" of the system. They believed these offenders should have their cases reviewed and sentences reduced. In fact, they had put their beliefs into practice and were due to release many of these drug offenders in 2016.

Realize that national politics play a role in the cases that the U.S. attorney's will prosecute. Just because there are laws on the books, it doesn't mean they will be enforced.

Ensure that you are aware of the politics in your jurisdiction and in the jurisdictions that may partner with you in a task force. Knowing the politics may alleviate misunderstandings early in the investigative process and allow you to plan appropriately.

5

Formalize Task Force

Once you find the right people to work with and the working group has been together for a while, there will be a time to formalize the working group into a task force.

A formal federal task force has many benefits. Some of the perks include overtime for local officers and official oversight. This may help you ensure that the best officers are dedicated to the task force.

In Chapter 6, we will describe the different types of federal task forces. We will also look at some of the avenues available to federal agents leading a working group of local law enforcement departments looking for assistance from federal task forces that may already exist in their jurisdiction.

Whether the original working group is two officers from two departments or 30 officers from several different federal, state, and local law enforcement agencies, the time will come when it is obvious to evolve into a formal task force.

Some of the factors that contribute to that evolution are the size and scope of the crime problem. Is this an issue that can quickly be resolved by the actions of the existing working group? Or is it going to be a protracted long-term investigative effort? Is there a limitation on resources of the working group?

Some departments will not allow their officers to devout too much time to an informal working group but will assign officers to a task force that is paying overtime and providing additional resources to their department's efforts. Other law enforcement agencies may have political reasons that a working group is better for them. For others, the politics will lean toward a formal task force. Gauge and measure the law enforcement circumstances that exist within the scope of your crime problem. Be wise with your requests and address the needs of the participating law enforcement agencies.

An advantage to initiating a working group prior to formalizing into a task force is the time spent with the working group allows the leader to evaluate the members of the working group. You get to know the people that you will be working with prior to the formalized task force. Are the participants the types of people you want working on the formal task force?

Although the working group allows you to conduct an informal evaluation of your counterparts, a formal task force usually requires input during their year-end reviews. A personnel evaluation of the people assigned to a formal task force is usually done by the lead federal agency. The parent agency will ask the lead agent for annual input regarding their officer's individual performance. In a working group, the informal atmosphere doesn't require evaluation of the people assigned; however, workers are workers. The slackers in the working group aren't going to become ball of fire investigators just because the working group is formalized into a task force.

The bottom line is to keep your eyes open. Recognize the capabilities of the people assigned to your working group. Ensure that they are worth your while. Remember, these will be the same people you will have as members of a formal task force that you have to maintain.

An additional benefit that comes with formalizing a task force is the assignment of a federal prosecutor. If the investigation is deserving of a dedicated federal prosecutor, a formalized task force is the appropriate avenue to obtain one. Further recompense to a formal federal task force is the state and local police officers are sworn in as federal officers by the U.S. Marshals Service. Once deputized and sworn in, they receive credentials and have federal arrest powers.

Remember, the assessment of the crime problem and projected resolutions should be documented. They also should be analyzed to determine what best course of action addresses the needs of the public. Circumstances will change from one crime problem to another; resolution depends on the crime problem, the current situation, and resource availability of participating departments.

Let's examine the roles of the agencies that may be invited to participate in your working group and/or task force.

The federal agencies that would have jurisdiction and would be considered as primary partners in the working group would be, the Federal Bureau of Investigation (FBI). The FBI would investigate what criminal activity the criminal organizations are committing locally and regionally. They also would investigate what other crimes they are involved in on an interstate or international level.

The Drug Enforcement Agency (DEA) has primary investigative responsibility for narcotics trafficking.

The Bureau of Alcohol, Tobacco, Firearms and Explosives (ATF) investigates firearms violations.

The U.S. Postal Office may also have an investigative interest as major cartels may use the postal service to launder and ship money.

If investigation shows an avenue into the U.S. military, then the U.S. Army's Criminal Investigations Division (CID) and the U.S. Navy's Naval Criminal Investigative Service (NCIS) may be interested in joining the working group as primary or secondary partners.

The Immigration and Naturalization Service (INS) would be a good secondary partner if the investigation shows involvement in illegal aliens.

The U.S. Probation Office can be a great ancillary partner to any law enforcement working group, as the investigation progresses and subjects are identified that may be on federal probation.

The Internal Revenue Service (IRS) is also a valuable asset to investigate tax evasion charges on enterprise leaders.

Initial coordination between federal agencies when addressing a new crime problem is vital.

It is important to involve the U.S. attorneys from any judicial districts that may have jurisdiction. The coordination of a major investigation through the appropriate U.S. Attorney's Office cannot be underemphasized. The entire investigation will hinge on the early involvement of an assistant U.S. attorney (AUSA) and the quality of the AUSA assigned.

An AUSA who is engaged in the investigation and who can be reached at 3 o'clock in the morning to obtain federal search and arrest warrants is an essential component to success. There will be an entire Chapter 7 devoted to prosecutors later in this book. The AUSA assigned to the working group as it morphs into a task force will always have the endgame prosecutions in mind. It is imperative the lead investigators and lead AUSA be on the same sheet of music with the same goals and objectives.

The next step is to examine what state, county, and local law enforcement agencies have jurisdiction and may wish to be involved in the working group and/or task force. Inviting the appropriate state and local law enforcement agencies to address a crime problem through the working group and/or task force is a critical decision point in the investigation process. Take in to account the issues previously discussed.

Local law enforcement usually provides the bulk of the personnel assigned to a task force; ensure that they have a dog in the fight when addressing the current crime problem. In other words, do not embellish or oversell the task at hand.

If the crime problem can be resolved through individual federal prosecutions and state and local charges, a formalized task force may not be necessary. An informal working group may be sufficient to accomplish the mission.

6

Types of Task Forces

In this chapter, we will discuss the various types of task forces that are available to investigators.

When I first started working cases in 1986, formalized task forces were in their fledgling stages. When I reported to Seattle, the only formalized task force at the time was the Green River Killer Task Force. During that period, the common practice was that local FBI agents often partnered up with local detectives on an informal basis. They worked together on cases with joint venue, rather than formalizing into a task force. Most FBI agents had close law enforcement contacts in the local police departments. We were truly "partners." We trusted them and they trusted us.

This informal practice was efficient. When a major crime such as a kidnapping occurred, we came together and addressed the problem. When the problem was resolved we would go our separate ways until the next major case.

As a new agent, I teamed up with a Pierce County Sheriff's detective. He was an experienced investigator. I learned a lot of basic field techniques from working with him. The basics skills included interviewing subjects, suspects, and witnesses. I had been taught these techniques in new agents training, but honing these skills in the field was crucial to reach a level of competence in interviewing people. Training is great but nothing beats experience. Getting people to talk to you is the true measure of a good investigator.

By the time I was transferred to Los Angeles in late 1990, the task force concept was catching on and gaining momentum. In the early 1990s,

FBI Los Angeles had several bank robbery task forces in Los Angeles and several satellite offices.

During that period, I was assigned to the West Covina Resident Agency (WCRA). The WCRA is a satellite office of the FBI Los Angeles Division. The WCRA started a bank robbery task force with the Los Angeles Sheriff's Office (LASO). Unfortunately, many local law enforcement agencies didn't send their best and brightest to these early task forces. They saw it as an opportunity to drop their deadweight on the feds. The deputy sent to the WCRA's bank robbery task force was a dud. He would sit in the office and read fiction novels at his desk.

At a time when the WCRA was getting 400 bank robberies a year, we were required to respond to every bank robbery and conduct a complete investigation. We were busy as hell. Having a detective who wasn't pulling his weight was very divisive. One who would only respond to a bank robbery when physically threatened was very problematic.

Owing to politics, the FBI supervisor was hesitant to ask the LASO for a replacement. However, that changed rapidly when the LASO deputy used his leased FBI car to transport cages of live chickens. The ensuing fiasco covered the back seat of FBI-leased vehicle with feathers and chicken shit. The FBI supervisor finally had enough and asked for a new deputy.

Owing to the humiliating situation, the LASO agreed and replaced the original deputy. I will give them credit. The replacement they sent over was a very competent deputy. He pulled his weight. He worked hard to fit in with us on the task force.

The lesson for the day is if a task force member from a department is a problem, talk to them. Make every effort, and try to get through to them that you won't tolerate bad behavior. If they don't change ask their department for a replacement. Even if the department pulls their support for the task force, it will be better for your overall mission than allowing a glaring malignancy to grow (Table 6.1).

OK, let's look at what task force options would be available to us as a federally backed working group looking to formalize into a task force. As you can see in Table 6.1, there are several options available to federal agencies and to state and local officials looking for assistance in addressing emerging crime problems. Each task force has specific funding and resource options available to investigators.

One that I had mentioned earlier was the Organized Crime and Drug Enforcement Task Force (OCDETF). Initiation requires the OCDETF case must have a nexus to drug trafficking. The local U.S. Attorney's

Table 6.1 Task Force Options

Name of Task Force	Type	Lead Agency	Description
Organized Crime and Drug Enforcement Task Force (OCDETF)	Drug	Any federal agency	OCDETF is a drug task force that requires one federal agency partner, usually case specific
High Intensity Drug Trafficking Areas (HIDTA)	Drug	DEA, FBI	HIDTA is a more permanent drug task force that has multiple drug case in a region; designed to address high drug trafficking areas
Safe Streets and Gang Task Forces (SSTF)	Gang	FBI	Gang-specific task force run by the FBI; designed to target gang problems locally and regionally
Project Safe Neighborhoods (PSN)	Guns	ATF	Task force specific to gun cases run by the ATF; designed to address gun-related crimes
Fugitive Task Force	Fugitive	U.S. Marshal	U.S. Marshal Task Force designed to apprehend fugitives

Office runs an OCDETF committee that reviews requests and approves OCDETF proposals. The FBI, DEA, ATF, U.S. Marshals Service, IRS, and Immigration and Customs Enforcement (ICE) are usually members of the U.S. Attorney-led OCDETF committee.

The advantages of an OCDETF are an assigned AUSA and some overtime payments to your local departments that are members of the task force. The OCDETF prerequisites are simple. A federal agency member teams up with at least one local or state agency and authors a proposal for the OCDETF committee review. The proposals are standardized and electronically fillable on a computer.

The OCDETF is a good avenue to take on early in a criminal enterprise investigation. It allows investigators to formalize and tap into assets such as analysts and administrative assistance. It also comes with an assigned AUSA. Another benefit is freedom for your task force to grow.

Formalizing into OCDETF will not prohibit you from establishing a Safe Streets and Gang Task Forces (SSTF) or any other task force. The OCDETF case can be investigated on a parallel path. OCDETF evidence and charges can be incorporated into the task force investigation.

The High Intensity Drug Trafficking Areas (HIDTA) Task Forces provide assistance in the form of intelligence and information-sharing initiatives. HIDTA offers support for programs that provide assistance beyond the core enforcement. HIDTA also includes drug use prevention and drug treatment initiatives. These services are provided to federal, state, local, and tribal law enforcement agencies operating in areas determined to be critical drug trafficking regions of the United States.

Unlike OCDETFs that address drug cases in any area where there is a problem, HIDTA was formed to address problems in areas determined to be high drug trafficking. If your crime problem is in one of these HIDTA, and it is drug trafficking, HIDTA is an excellent option to engage as a task force option.

Yet, if you are investigating a crime problem not directly related to the HIDTA primary mission, their intelligence sharing initiatives may still be a resource that can be utilized by your working group or task force. If your criminal enterprise is involved in narcotics trafficking in a HIDTA, coordination with the HIDTA group is highly recommended.

In the early 1990s, the FBI organized the Safe Streets Violent Crime Initiative, to address street crime at a national level. The FBI formed the SSGU at FBIHQ to oversee the gang program. The SSGU has program management responsibilities for the Safe Streets and Gang Task Forces (SSTF). The SSTF was designed to allow each FBI field office to address violent street gangs and drug-related violence through the establishment of FBI sponsored, long-term, proactive task forces focusing on violent gangs, crime of violence, and the apprehension of violent fugitives.

The SSTFs became the vehicle through which federal, state, and local law enforcement agencies joined together to address the violent crime plaguing their communities. They pursue violent gangs through sustained, proactive, coordinated investigations to obtain prosecutions under the USC, Titles 18 and 21, including violations such as racketeering, drug conspiracy, and firearms violations.

The SSTF concept expands cooperation and communication among federal, state, and local law enforcement agencies, increasing productivity and avoiding duplication of investigative efforts.

If you have a crime problem that involves a sophisticated criminal enterprise that requires more effort and resources that you have with an OCDETF, and there is not sufficient drug trafficking to solicit HIDTA support, the SSTF is a good next step for to expand and formalize your task force. The SSGU will pay overtime to your local and state officers and supply them vehicles. Check with the SSGU for current benefits and requirements of the SSTFs.

Currently, the U.S. Marshals Service leads 60 local Fugitive Task Forces across the country. The majority of the task forces are full-time efforts; however, additional task forces are formed on an ad hoc basis, in response to specific cases.

Funding for these Fugitive Task Forces is often granted through initiatives such as the HIDTA, OCDETF, and Project Safe Neighborhoods (PSN) Task Forces.

The Fugitive Task Forces are good resources if you identify the subjects of your criminal enterprise already have warrants. If your crime problem consists of a crew that already has warrants for felonies that will disrupt their activities and dismantle their operations, initiate or engage a Fugitive Task Force for quick and effective results.

Even if you decide to initiate another type of task force, establish a good working relationship with any existing Fugitive Task Force in your area. They can arrest potential sources and suspects for you in the future. If missions do not conflict, the Fugitive Task Force can be a valuable ally that can provide a surge of resources when needed.

PSN is a nationwide commitment to reduce gun crime in America by networking existing local programs that target gun crime and providing those programs with additional tools to fit the specific gun crime problems in each area. The goal is to create safer neighborhoods by reducing gun violence and sustaining that reduction through supporting prosecution of firearms-related offenses.

Similar to the Fugitive Task Forces, coordination with any PSN in your territory will be crucial for intelligence and resource management avenues. The ATF is usually the main federal agency leading the PSN Task Forces.

In the NLR case, the FBI Riverside Resident Agency formed the "Wood Buster" Task Force as an OCDETF. Members of the task force were FBI agents, SSU agents of the CDC and Ontario Police Department officers. Later, we added the Upland and Fontana Police Departments. We also worked with the ATF as an ancillary member of the task force. We also did become an FBI SSTF and supplied cars and overtime to our officers.

35

Whether you are a new federal agent or a state and local law enforcement department addressing a crime problem, there are a myriad of task force options available to you to explore and decide which avenue is right for your working group. There are other resources available to state and local law enforcement such as federal grants to address various crime problems.

The U.S. Department of Justice has a website available to law enforcement to explore funding and assistance (http://ojp.gov/programs/lawenforcement.htm).

7

Prosecutors

There is an old fishing adage, "I'll catch them, if you clean them." This saying is a good way to explain the relationship between the prosecutors and investigators in a major task force investigation.

A team of the best investigators in the world, gathering the best evidence ever collected on the most violent criminal enterprise that ever existed, is nothing more than intelligence if the prosecutors decline to charge the subjects of the investigation. The end game is to dismantle the criminal enterprise, and it can't be done without effective prosecution.

The importance of a prosecutor to the overall mission to disrupt and dismantle the targeted criminal enterprise cannot be overemphasized.

A good working relationship between prosecutors and investigators must be established and maintained on a daily basis. When I say prosecutors, I mean prosecutors at both the federal and local levels.

Even if the investigation is destined as a federal RICO case that will eventually be prosecuted in the federal court, there will be a crucial components of the investigation that will include state and local charges on the subjects, associates, and family members of the targeted criminal enterprise.

Some of these charges will be local, and state charges based upon the task force direct investigation and other state charges will be brought by other law enforcement agencies. Since the subjects of your criminal enterprise will be criminals, they are going to commit crimes.

Trust me when I say your task force will not be aware or be capable to investigate every crime they commit. So, be prepared. By briefing local district attorneys of your investigation, you may engage them to assist you. If they are aware and involved, they may call you if your subjects end up being arrested by another law enforcement agency.

There will also be crimes that do not reach the federal prosecutive level but can be charged in state court. These charges against your subjects, their enemies, associates, allies, potential informants, or others will play into the disruption phase of the investigation.

A good working relationship with the district attorney also comes into play if your existing or potential informants are arrested. (Yes, your informants are crooks, and they will be arrested.) Making a deal with a potential informant on existing criminal charges is a primary motivator in informant development.

With prior coordination, the district attorney may be judicious if a "deal" needs to be made regarding your subjects, to elicit their cooperation. Having a hammer to hold over informants as they cooperate in the investigation is as good as a guarantee as it gets. The written formal plea agreement is the best avenue to ensure that the informants will do what you are asking them to do and not going sideways on you.

Having a district attorney assigned to the task force is the best-case scenario. If it is someone that your local cops know, all the better. It will give a definite edge through the course of your investigation.

As for the U.S. Attorney's Office, let me start out by saying, as a former FBI agent, I cannot tell you the number of times I would have liked to physically choke the living hell out of an AUSA.

For example, I spent nine months investigating a slave trafficking ring that was transporting female teenagers from Seattle to Los Angeles for prostitution. The Mann Act made it a felony to engage in interstate or foreign commerce transport of "any woman or girl for the purpose of prostitution or debauchery, or for any other immoral purpose." The main subject had transported nine different females from Seattle to Los Angeles over a period of two years. In my nine-month investigation, I interviewed each of the victims and their family members, found hotel records in Los Angeles to back each of their stories, and got a confession from the subject.

The AUSA I was working with drafted an indictment for 18 counts of violation of the Mann Act. The subject was looking at 30 years in prison. Nonetheless, without even telling me, the AUSA allowed the subject to plead guilty to one count. The subject got five years. I was shocked and angered by his unilateral decision. The prosecutive opinion was the AUSA's prerogative, of course, but the way he handled it ensured that I never wanted to work with him again.

There were several other examples of arrogance, malaise, and just pure laziness in my 25 years in dealing with AUSAs in several federal judicial districts.

On the other end of the spectrum, I think it is best to move on and talk about some great AUSAs that I worked with. There were two AUSAs that I worked with that I would walk through fire for and would work with again today. AUSA Charlene Olmedo was the lead AUSA on the NLR case in Los Angeles, California. AUSA Dan Graber and I worked counter-terrorism matters and mortgage fraud together in Madison, Wisconsin.

Some common trait of these AUSAs was passion and total engagement in the mission. They believed in what we were doing. They thought the prosecutions they prepared were the right thing to do, a cause to believe in. They understood that the investigations and prosecutions were necessary to bring down the targeted criminal enterprises. Passion and engagement is critical for all task force members, including the AUSAs.

Everyone working in the task force understood that the leaders of these criminal organizations were operating with impunity and would continue to do so unless we dismantled their criminal enterprises.

AUSA Olmedo was already assigned to the NLR case by the time I came on board the investigation. She was hardworking and down to earth. It wasn't long before I was calling her several times a day with prosecutive opinions regarding subjects that we were investigating. She was responsive to our investigative needs, even in the middle of the night. If we needed an arrest warrant or a search warrant, she would answer the call and respond immediately.

I was careful not to waste her time or take advantage of her aggressive prosecutive nature. She and I became partners in the strategic overview of the NLR case. We developed and executed on the long-term dismantlement strategy by using RICO prosecutions on the NLR leaders. We also used all charges for the disruption of NLR daily operations with the arrests of their operatives and seizure of their drugs and assets.

She knew her job and I knew mine, and together we formed an effective team. We never argued about roles and responsibilities. We did have some back and forth discussions on some cases. Mostly about if we had enough evidence to charge a subject, but if there wasn't enough, she would tell me what we needed and we would continue to investigate. It was a pleasure and honor working with her. I would do it again in a heartbeat.

The other stellar AUSA worked with me on a sensitive counter-terrorism investigation that I cannot discuss here. Nevertheless, I will say that Dan Graber was the most aggressive AUSA that I ever worked with and was also the smartest.

Unlike the NLR AUSA, I had some contentious interactions with this Dan on the counterterrorism case. There was some initial confusion on the roles and responsibilities between us, as investigators and prosecutors. We eventually worked through this diversity together. We clearly defined our roles, and with responsibilities defined, our problems were solved.

In later years, Dan and I worked together addressing mortgage fraud in Wisconsin. Through planning meetings, we developed a strategy to investigate and prosecute lenders, brokers, and borrowers if they knowingly produced, processed, and completed fraudulent loan applications.

With our roles and responsibilities clearly established up front, we set to work. We were successful in our efforts. We indicted and convicted several mortgage brokers that knowingly processed fraudulent loan applications for borrowers. We also convicted several borrowers that obtained loans through fraudulent loan applications and then defaulted on those loans because they couldn't pay their mortgages.

The bottom line is the prosecutors will be key to the success or failure of your investigative efforts. Different U.S. Attorneys' Offices have different rules for case assignment. In some districts you can solicit the AUSAs directly with cases and in some you can't; find out the normal practice in your district and play by their rules. Although you may not always be able to select the AUSA for your case, there are avenues to get AUSAs that you know and have worked with in the past to ask their supervisors to assign them to your investigation.

The AUSA should be your closest ally in any criminal enterprise investigation. Ensure that everyone understands his or her roles and responsibilities early on in the investigation to minimize conflict at a later and more crucial date.

8

Basic Training

One of the key facets of a Safe Streets Task Force is the enterprise theory of investigation (ETI). The strategy of ETI calls for the combining of short-term, street-level enforcement activity and sophisticated techniques as consensual monitoring, financial analysis, and Title III wire intercepts investigations. Using ETI is designed to root out and prosecute the entire gang.

This type of investigation includes cases on the street-level thugs and dealers up through the crew leaders and ultimately the gang's command structure. The ETI has proven time and again how effective federal racketeering, drug conspiracy, and firearms investigations are in targeting a criminal enterprise. Whether the goal of the specific investigation is to provide incentive for witnesses to cooperate or imprisoning the gang's leaders for decades, the ETI is an effective tool for task force investigators.

Besides the investigation of and disruption of street-level operations, the ETI utilizes RICO, VICAR, CCE, firearms charges, and sophisticated investigative techniques to target and dismantle a criminal enterprise. These sophisticated investigative techniques include communication intercepts (commonly referred to as "wiretaps") and undercover activities.

The use of these techniques is unique to each and every investigation and should only be used in appropriate situations.

Before working group members could participate in the more advanced sophisticated investigative techniques, they must be evaluated and trained in basic investigative techniques. Interviewing, report writing, evidence collection, and basic investigative skills must be set to a high standard. All agents and officers must meet those standards.

Evaluate assigned personnel in the basic skills and assess training needs for the entire task force staff. There will be times that they will do things differently. They learned to do things in a different system. Ensure that they understand the standards set for the task force. You must establish and maintain a high standard, but you must also ensure those standards are understood by all the members of the task force.

For instance, I recall an occasion when we had recovered four firearms from a subject's residence that had prior felony convictions. There were other people in the house and the subject denied possession or any knowledge of the firearms. I observed a couple of the task force officers handling the firearms without gloves. I asked why they weren't wearing gloves. The response was "Oh we never get fingerprints off guns. We don't even process them for fingerprints anymore."

I put on some gloves and bagged the guns myself. I took the guns and had them processed for fingerprints. Through the FBI lab, I got a match on the main subject's fingerprints on two of the four firearms. We charged him with federal felony in possession of a firearm. Since the subject was facing 10 years in federal prison, he chose to become a cooperating witness. The officers I was working with were impressed.

I used this as a training point. From that moment on, all task force members used gloves when handling firearms. All firearms were processed for fingerprints. The change was well received and successful. We did have other successes regarding firearms and fingerprints.

Working group and/or task force members must receive training in the basic investigative techniques relate to the lead investigative agency.

For example, if you have experienced detectives from a major police department assigned to an FBI SSTF, they will be used to writing reports in the first person, while the FBI writes reports in the third person. Not that there is anything wrong with either technique, but the standardization of reporting in a long-term investigation has great value to the future prosecution. If a formalized task force take on a criminal enterprise that will be prosecuted under the RICO statute, the investigation may go on for years. Standardization of report writing is a good tool to begin training of task force officers and help them understand the value of the long-term investigation.

Training of working group or task force members must be handled diplomatically and with respect for all personnel. Most people will not admit when they are not comfortable with a subject in which everyone else seems competent. Nobody likes to be told that they aren't up to snuff, and that they need additional training. The finesse comes with identifying areas where everyone needs training and areas where individuals may needs assistance. If the whole group needs training, then give it to them.

However, there may be instances where it is more appropriate to pull an officer or agent aside and provide them discreet individual training. The more sensitive training sessions comes with mentoring individuals that may need additional training in basic investigative techniques.

Make no mistake; the basic investigative training evaluation must be made across all task force members, federal state, and local law enforcement officers. Just because an FBI agent has 10 years of service, it doesn't mean that the agent has been investigating cases for that entire time. Since 2001, the FBI has concentrated a lot of effort on intelligence collection and developed career paths for agents outside the traditional criminal investigative agent. Some of them may have never interviewed a criminal subject before. Know your people, all your people.

Each task force will have a different personality based upon the people assigned. A good leadership tool is to find people's strengths and assign them to areas where they can utilize their skills in a positive manner that allows them to contribute to the mission.

The rewards to the individuals will come from knowing their work mattered and assisted the task force. Find out who is good at what and give them the tools to do their job. There will be people that excel at evidence collection but are not comfortable at interviewing subjects. There is always a scrounger that gets resources for the task force when no one else could. How about the officer that can turn any subject into an informant?

Just make sure they are focused on the overall mission, set the ground rules, and monitor their progress.

In the NLR Task Force, I faced the problem of task force officers understanding and participating in the dismantlement phase of the NLR through RICO charges. We had decided to attack the NLR with a two-pronged attack. The first prong depended on disruption of their daily operations through the enforcement of street crimes on their associates and drug labs. The second prong was the dismantlement of NLR leadership through RICO charges.

The local cops were very familiar with the enforcement of the street crimes and taking down the drug labs. They were comfortable "running and gunning," working various street crimes. We were on the streets every day and night. Besides, it was fun, and I enjoyed it as much as they did.

However, investigating the RICO charges took a lot of boring days, weeks, months, and years reviewing old case files on NLR leadership to identify two counts (on each person) that the AUSA could use in the RICO prosecution.

AUSA Olmedo began the RICO effort with comprehensive classes to all task force members on the RICO statute and the burden of proof for predicate acts. In the RICO statute, you not only have to prove the offense was committed by the subject but also have to prove it was done for the furtherance of the organization.

The rewards were long term, but not as satisfying as busting an NLR drug lab or arresting an NLR member with a gun and charging him with ex-felon in possession of a firearm. Digging through boxes of old files, then running across California and Nevada, visiting godforsaken prisons and jails looking for evidence for possible murders, attempted murders, assaults, and other RICO-related offenses was time consuming, boring, and hard work. The local cops didn't want to do it.

So, to overcome this problem, I established a compromise. In the five-day work week, the entire 12-person task force would spend two days a week working on the RICO charges. The other three days a week was spent enforcing street crimes. The compromise was successful and cut through divisive attitudes. We worked through the RICO charges but still got to run around and conduct the street enforcement.

Coming back to the matter at hand, a working group or task force will consist of several different levels of law enforcement, and even the departments of similar jurisdiction will have different ways of conducting investigations, writing and filing paperwork, and sometimes even conducting tactical operations.

It is imperative for officer safety that training with the group be conducted and done so at the highest standards. I demanded that all officers participating in any raids with the NLR Task Force wear their bullet-resistant vests. If they didn't have a personal vest, I bought some for them from FBI SSTF funds.

Another illustration concerning officer safety was firearms training. The FBI qualifies with assigned firearms every three months with qualification being a score of 80 out of a possible 100 on the 50-round pistol course. Some of the smaller departments that I worked with only qualified with their firearms once a year, and the qualification was an 18-round course. Every task force that I led qualified with their firearms every three months with the FBI office firearms instructors. I set a high standard, including for firearms qualification.

I would also make the task force members wore their bullet-resistant vest when they shot on the range. I ensured that every task force member wore his or her vests when we went on a raid. They were resistant at first but when two of the officers who carried shotguns on raids had trouble shooting them with their vests on the range, they realized the safety issue. Imagine finding out you couldn't get your shot gun up to your shoulder and fire at a subject who was shooting at you. It was eye opening and a great training tool.

Another very valuable tool available to the SSTF was the weeklong task force training for SSTFs at the FBI Training Academy at Quantico, Virginia. The NLR Task Force attended as a group. We stayed in the barracks together, ate together, and ran through arrest scenarios together. It was a valuable tool to evaluate the level of proficiency of all the task force members and also see different ways of tackling a problem. Check with the SSGU to see if they are still running that program. If available, I highly recommend it.

The bottom line is as the leader of the task force effort, get to know your people and their levels of competency in basic criminal investigation techniques and get them the training they need. Once trained, get them the experience that bolsters their investigative skills. Get them out and have them investigate; monitor their progress. Be patient. Remember we all had to start somewhere.

9

Engage Community

There has always been a division and lack of trust between law enforcement and many social service community groups. But trust me when I say, church groups, youth groups, housing authority, and other community services have a place in your task force investigation.

The division comes from varying points of view between law enforcement officials and social workers. The law enforcement point of view is that the citizenry must be protected at all costs. They believe there are certain members of society who are criminals, and it is the job of the law enforcement officer to protect normal citizens from these predators. With numbers showing that 15% of the population conducts 90% of the crime, they have a point. There are people out there who are criminals. Regardless of how they got to be what they are, they are not likely to change their behavior.

The other point of view is the social worker. They often believe that there is no such thing as a bad kid. Social workers believe that criminals are the product of a poor socioeconomic environment and only turn to crime due to necessity. They also believe if society improved the social class of the poor community the crime rate would be reduced by the numbers of criminals that would either go straight or be productive citizens through choice.

My first job in my law enforcement career was as a corrections officer in the Clark County Detention Facility in Las Vegas, Nevada. I dealt with some pretty bad customers and hardened criminals. I developed some rigid views on criminals. I believed that once they went bad, they weren't coming back. In some cases, I still believe that there are some bad people out there.

Nevertheless, after investigating cases for 25 years in the FBI, I also developed a sense that there were some people that made mistakes and poor life choices. Because of their neighborhoods and/or peer pressure, these people made choices that put them in front of a law enforcement officer. After interviewing hundreds of criminals, my views have changed somewhat from my corrections officer days. Now I believe there could be some hope for this group of people, those who regret their bad life choices. I think that some of these people may change their direction through intervention by social programs that help them stay on the right path.

I found that by the time I interview a criminal as an FBI agent, they had already been through the youth authority, local jails, and state prison. By the time I was talking to them, I was preparing a case to send them to the federal prison. I realized that most of them were a lost cause. They had made it through the criminal justice education system: youth authority and jail was grade school, state prison was high school, and now they were going to college with federal time.

The likelihood of ever becoming a normal citizen faded with each higher level of this perverse criminal education. This class of people needs to be educated early in their criminal career and convinced to straighten out. That education point is where the social workers working with law enforcement may make a difference in some of these young lives. Many of these sad individuals wished they could speak to their youthful selves and set them on the right path.

Of course, this doesn't apply to every criminal I arrested. Some were just bad guys that would make the same evil choices repeatedly. If they had the advantage to speak to their youthful selves, the advice they would provide would be on how to conduct more and better criminal activity without being caught.

Unfortunately, we do not have national statistics on people who have the potential to be repeat offenders but were turned from a life of crime by a family member, clergyperson, school counselor, and so on. We also don't have specific character traits for a person that is going bad no matter what versus the person that could be turned. It comes down to personal decisions of potential criminals.

Because we can't differentiate between the good and the bad, there has to be community involvement across the board. Options must be made available outside the criminal career path. Education must be provided to all those vulnerable to recruitment by the criminal element. There must be a safe haven established for those who make the decisions to avoid contact with criminal element. These steps will not prevent all youth from embarking on a criminal career path but it may save a few.

Therefore, I encourage any law enforcement working group and/or task force to reach out to community social welfare groups and coordinate their investigative efforts with community leaders.

A good place to start is the local office of state welfare. They can provide an overview of active community leaders who will be active in the areas that contain the elements of the targeted criminal enterprise.

Initial contact with these leaders should set the tone if they will cooperate in the investigation or not. If they are interested, engage them and assist in educating vulnerable youths and encourage them to stay out of jail. Handcuffs on can be considered a great measure of success, your presentation may have got them to go straight.

OK, now I will take off my social worker hat and put my investigative fedora back on. There are other reasons to engage community leaders besides turning youth from a life of crime.

The community leaders will know the subjects of any criminal enterprises operating within their sphere of influence. They will know their operations, associates, enemies, and pretty much everything that you want to know as investigators. Make no mistake; the community leaders will possess a wealth of intelligence on the targeted enterprise. Having them on your side and cooperating would be a gold mine of real time intelligence. Eyes in the community are invaluable. Protect the information they give you and build a personal trust with the community leaders.

However, the avenue of educating and deflecting youth is a real mission, not just an inroad to the community leader. Do not utilize this valuable tool as an insincere effort to work the community leaders as informants. Be sincere, honest, and truthful with them and treat them with respect. If you don't they will find you out and the investigation will suffer.

Besides, as a law enforcement officer, you started a career to always do the right thing. Do not lose sight of your own career path.

Section II

Intelligence

10

Develop an Organizational Chart

As the hawkers selling program player rosters at the baseball game yell, "Get your programs here. You can't tell the players without a program." Concentrate efforts on identifying key players in your targeted criminal enterprise. Who are the leaders? Who are the mid-level managers? Who are the low-level players? Associates? Family members? (Figure 10.1).

Early in the investigation, document key intelligence regarding the overall criminal enterprise and continue to update the documents throughout the investigation. The amount of information you accrue over the course of a three-year investigation could be massive. Always be prepared. Preparation starts with organization and documentation of significant milestones in your investigation. Ensure that the documentation is searchable for future use in the investigation.

Start by identifying everyone connected to your criminal enterprise in any way imaginable. This sounds very generic but you have to start somewhere and the minion of today is often the leader of tomorrow. Put their names in an organizational chart that can be manipulated with changes that occur on a daily basis.

At first, a pad of paper and those giant post-it pads will suffice. But as the investigation grows, it is highly recommended that the task force invest in some investigative software that is easy to update and malleable enough to display several organizational charts at one time. It should also have a search capability to cross refer names, phone numbers, addresses, car license plates, and other pertinent investigative data.

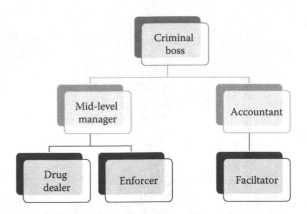

Figure 10.1 Example of an organizational chart.

Eventually, investigation will begin to sort through the roles of the members. Within a relatively short period, the people running the enterprise will become clear.

With that being said, single out the leaders of the criminal enterprise. These are the people that are issuing orders to the criminal enterprise. The leaders are the people that issues orders, which are actually being followed. Criminal acts are being committed because of those orders. Identify the people critical to the organization because of their leadership and oversight, those that drive the organization. Without them, the organization cannot function. Develop an organizational chart with a defined structure and links between those displayed on the organizational chart.

Once initially documented, keep in mind that the organizational chart will change. During the course of the investigation, new leaders will be identified, and old leaders will be arrested or killed. Things will change and the organizational charts should keep up with those changes as close to real time as possible.

Throughout the course of the investigation, ensure the leaders are the targets of the RICO or most serious charges. They will bear the brunt of the dismantlement phase of the task force investigation. The goal is to dismantle the criminal enterprise by putting the leaders in prison for long terms, thus enabling the enterprise to continue its operations.

Getting the leaders is a priority, but do not lose sight of the fact that almost all organizations depend on mid-level managers to run the organizations on a daily basis. The direction, vision, and strategic thinking are usually done at the leadership level but the implementation of the vision of the leader of any organization is carried out by the mid-level manager's oversight of the working-level personnel. The disruption phase of the investigation will target the mid-level managers and street-level criminals that make the operation run.

Charges levied against these individuals for any violation is a good strategy to disrupt the criminal enterprise operations and to explore the possibility of informant development. The value of a mid-level member who knows the criminal enterprise operations intimately and is willing to testify in the federal grand jury is very impactful.

With this in mind, every interview that is conducted with subjects willing to speak to you about their charges must include a solicitation to become a cooperating witness. When conducting the initial interview, ensure you obtain an admission of their guilt to the charges that you have on them. Remember that is your first priority. If they agree to cooperate, after proper *Miranda* warnings, discuss their value with the AUSA. Then carefully choose those that will be offered a deal to reduce their charges. Your second priority is to gain their cooperation on the criminal enterprise.

Never promise them anything. Tell them any deal is up to the AUSA. The deal depends on the value of their information. Ask them what they know about the organization and its members, and obtain a detailed debriefing. Tell them you will validate their information and consult with the AUSA.

In the NLR case, we practiced this on every worthy subject, always in consultation with AUSA Olmedo. If we interviewed a subject that had knowledge of NLR activities and criminal acts and they agreed to cooperate, we would have the subject testifying in front of a federal grand jury within two or three days, depending on the day of the week they were arrested. Ideally, it would be the next day. The evidence of an insider's testimony in the federal grand jury is very powerful evidence in any future trials. It also locks in the subject's testimony. It is easy to dispute a police report or FBI FD302 report form as the officer's or agent's opinion, but much more difficult to refute federal grand jury transcripts (or tapes) in their own words.

Identifying the people who are working in your targeted criminal enterprise is a high priority. Knowing who they are and what their roles and responsibilities are in the organization will determine how you investigate each individual identified. Putting together and maintaining an organizational chart of your subjects will allow you to develop the program roster of the targeted criminal enterprise essential to success of your task force investigation.

OK, where do you start? How do you find out who your bad guys are and how are they connected? Obviously, there has to be a starting point. Gather your working group or task force members and start writing names on the blackboard of subjects that they know and how they know them. Informants? Prior arrests? Interviews? Police reports? News reporting? Past investigations? Any subject matter experts on the criminal enterprise from law enforcement in the local area?

Throw the names out there and start putting them in an organizational chart. Do you have any leaders identified? If you have a name of any leader identified, start with him or her.

Once you identify a leader, find their telephone numbers, and get a subpoena for their past six months of toll records. Review the toll records. Determine if they are utilizing their telephone to conduct business to run their criminal enterprise. The telephone records could be a gold mine that you can use to map out their contacts.

Do they have a legitimate job? How about finances? Obtain a subpoena for bank records for the targeted leader. Analyze the records for income, what is coming in? Who are they paying?

As you develop evidence and can show the telephones are being used for criminal activity, the use of pen registers to capture telephone numbers as they are made should seriously be considered.

This investigative pathway may lead your task force to the utilization of a Title III wiretap on your subject's smartphone. If the subjects are communicating openly using their smartphone, the evidence collection leads your investigation to a quick and successful conclusion.

Being an old geezer, we did not have Facebook, LinkedIn, Twitter, or any other social media venue when we were working cases in the 1980s or 1990s. But I wish we would have had them. The amount of information that can be gleaned from a social media account is utterly amazing. The best thing about these accounts is they are public information; anyone can see them.

An undercover account that cannot be traced back to law enforcement is simple enough to initiate. Check with you AUSA or department legal counsel to obtain the rules for your department regarding social media. If your legal advisor approves you to open a covert social media account, open one and utilize it to cruise your subject's Facebook account and document their friends section. Criminal background checks on the subject's friends will tell you if they have criminal records. Exploring any method of communication the subject may be utilizing will only benefit and further the investigation.

Any name and data gathered should be entered into a searchable database for future retrieval. As an experienced investigator, I have found that initial information may seem unimportant or unworthy of entry into a database, but upon review may become a valuable piece of evidence on a targeted leader.

For example, I recall one occasion where we were on surveillance at a house that we eventually raided and shut down an NLR methamphetamine lab. Various vehicles came and went during the course of our surveillance. We meticulously recorded license plates of the vehicles and descriptions of occupants. At the end of the surveillance the log was entered into our database, along with license plates and subject descriptions. We charged the people at the scene of the drug lab but they did not initially cooperate. We did not tie a NLR leader to the drug lab until sometime later when we identified one of the vehicles from the first surveillance showed up at the surveillance of another drug lab.

It just so happened that the same officer was on the surveillance log that day and noticed the vehicle before we even got back to the office. It turned out that the vehicle belonged to a meth cooker who worked for the NLR and other gangs in Los Angeles.

Although arrested, he would not cooperate. He didn't have to; his presence at these residences was enough for us to identify him. His arrest hampered the NLR's ability to run their meth operations, thereby disrupting their operations.

The point is keep track of the collected information. It may be more valuable tomorrow that today but only if you can review it again.

The names, contact numbers, social media, and financial information gathered on any leader will undoubtedly identify other members of the targeted criminal enterprise. The process will be repeated many times as you identify subjects, associates, partners, and family members of the targeted criminal enterprise.

Whether you choose to go overt or covert with your investigation, identify the leaders and the middle-level subjects that get things done. Go after them with a passion and driven persistence.

11

Define Enterprise

This chapter will concentrate on collection, evaluation, and analysis of intelligence related to your targeted criminal enterprise.

Criminal intelligence is what you will use to define and dismantle a criminal enterprise. It involves the process of identifying their key players and defining what kind of criminal activity they are conducting. These steps along with the statutes you will use to arrest and charge them, eventually dismantling their enterprise.

An important question that must be asked and answered is, "What is a criminal enterprise?"

There is a difference between two subjects entering into a conspiracy to commit a specific crime. The enterprise comes in when two guys who commit crimes contribute resources to a mutual partnership.

The legal definition on an enterprise is in the USC under the RICO statute: "enterprise" *includes any partnership, corporation, association, or other legal entity, and any union or group of individuals associated in fact although not a legal entity, which is engaged in, or the activities of which affect, interstate or foreign commerce.*

During the course of your investigation, the AUSA will ask you to prove the targets are engaged in an enterprise. This will be a requirement for them to prove to a jury to successfully prosecute RICO, CCE, or VICAR statutes. There are several ways to prove the organization you are investigating is an enterprise.

Testimony of members and leaders in the grand jury or in interviews regarding the organization is valuable evidence. However, written documentation by the criminal enterprise laying out their rules, articles of incorporation, or other written proof of their enterprise/organization, backing the testimony of cooperating witnesses, is the gold standard. One that is exceptional evidence is a standardized written code of conduct handed down by leaders. A code of conduct is a written document that outlines what the group is, believes in and how they expect members to act. Other evidence can be any documentation on rules of membership, such as requirements to join the group and punishments which can be expected by members for violating the rules.

Any documents and/or testimonies with orders from a ruling council calling for retribution against other groups or ex-members are also very valuable evidence.

Another point is to look to any known enemies of the targeted organization. If one organization is at war with another, then why not ally themselves with the federal government to get at their enemy? The cooperation of rival gang members could be invaluable to the investigation. The search for proof of the enterprise of your group will continue during the course of your investigation.

A portion of any interview with anyone associated with the targeted enterprise is how he or she knows the group is an enterprise. Develop and include simple standard questions regarding leadership, membership requirements, and written documentation in an interview guideline

Although defining a criminal enterprise may seem simple it is imperative. If defining the criminal enterprise is not addressed throughout the course of the investigation, the results could lead to the task force scrambling to prove the enterprise the week before an indictment. So take care of this task early on in the investigation and bolster throughout the entire investigative effort.

The structure and criminal enterprise of the NLR was identified and documented. Leaders of the NLR maintained control of the organization through intimidation and physical violence. If a prospect or junior member did not obey the orders of the "shot callers," he found his name was "put in the hat." This meant the NLR ordered other members to assault or kill him for his disobedience.

NLR leaders put a person on the NLR "hit list" (same as being put in the hat) for refusing to obey orders. Other violations calling for a "hit" were informing to the police, child molestation, unrecoverable drug debts, and not participating in a race riot or various other "rules" laid forth by the NLR. The NLR put forth these "hit lists" and circulated them through the organization. All NLR members are expected to kill anyone included on these lists, on sight.

The NLR had a flat structure with the leaders, called "seniors," able to call "shots (hits)," and sponsor new members. The most powerful senior would "hold the keys" (this term was kin to running a prison yard). Other NLR members obeyed the senior that "holds the keys." Seniors called shots under the area NLR leader but were required to obtain his permission before any "hits" are committed. Juniors and prospects were required to "put in work." This meant they were expected to commit assaults or murders, smuggle dope, and so on, until they became full-fledged members of the NLR. As a prospect conducts criminal activity for the NLR, he is sponsored by a senior until he becomes a full-fledged member. The more "work" a member puts into NLR business, the more powerful he becomes in the organization.

The initial NLR investigation led to the indictment of two NLR members with violation of the VICAR statute. The charges stemmed from the hate crime slashing (attempted murder) of a black inmate at the West Valley Detention Center. This incident validated the written white supremacist philosophy. The NLR committed hate crimes because of their philosophy. The NLR leader who ordered the slashing was indicted by a Federal Grand Jury on this charge and eventually convicted.

As you are defining the criminal enterprise, you will be collecting a massive amount of intelligence. A criminal intelligence analyst is a valuable resource and a good addition as a task force member. Still, good analysts are in high demand and most are assigned to fusion centers and not individual task forces.

Basic investigative techniques such as talking to people, gathering evidence, reviewing records (including criminal backgrounds) reviewing statutes are all basic intelligence collection techniques. They should be taught to and utilized by your task force officers.

Information gathered from these investigative techniques will develop intelligence, allowing the task force analysts, agents, and officers to outline the criminal enterprise's organizational chart, identify their patterns of criminal activity, and identify the enterprise's vulnerabilities and financial structure.

Knowing who is in your criminal enterprise and what kind of crimes they are committing is the most basic way to define criminal intelligence.

As the structure and criminal activity of the criminal enterprise are outlined, it will become clearer on which criminal statutes they are violating and will be investigated. If analysts are not available to the task force, the law enforcement officers must have the ability to collect, analyze, and evaluate criminal intelligence.

This is not as difficult as it sounds. In the 1980s, there were not many analysts available to FBI field agents. As FBI agents, we did most of the criminal intelligence analysis on our own. In the matter of defining the criminal enterprise, intelligence analysis is not that difficult.

As long as the task force remains focused on the mission to dismantle the criminal enterprise, the cases they investigate will gather criminal intelligence relevant to the criminal enterprise.

Problems arise when other criminal activity intelligence that distracts the task force from their primary mission is gathered. Mission focus is essential, as it is only natural to start running down leads on other criminal activity the task force will undoubtedly uncover while investigating the targeted enterprise.

If a task or criminal activity isn't related to the primary mission, the targeted criminal enterprise, the case must be handed off to another capable and interested law enforcement agency. Ensure any additional intelligence gathered is handed off to other law enforcement agencies with investigative interest in the ancillary intelligence.

Handing off a good case is an opportunity to establish or bolster liaison with other law enforcement agencies and/or task forces. Receiving unexpected but valuable information on a group that another task force or law enforcement agency has been investigating for a while is likely to allow you to form key alliances with those with whom you share the information.

Remember, criminal intelligence isn't magic; it is a matter of finding out who your crooks are and what criminal activity they are conducting. Then go after them by utilizing the statutes that give them the most time in prison. Disrupt and dismantle.

12

Research Criminal Activity

OK, as you have been defining the crime problem, you have identified some criminal activity, but now is the time you really have to evaluate what criminal activity the targeted criminal enterprise is heavily involved in on a daily basis.

What are they doing that is illegal? What is their primary source of income? Drugs? Taxes on drug dealers? Extortions? Robberies? White-collar crime? Prostitution?

There will be some criminal activity that is outside the umbrella of the criminal enterprise, some criminal activity that is conducted by a faction of the criminal enterprise or by individual members for individual profit. However, there will be criminal activity that is ingrained in the culture of the criminal enterprise. They will take pride in their work. This criminal activity may be hard for them to break away from; it is what they do, the bedrock of their criminal enterprise. They may evolve and change tactics to get around law enforcement pressure, but they will continue with this criminal activity.

For example, when we investigated them, the NLR drug of choice was methamphetamine. They liked to manufacture their own drugs and took pride in the high-quality crystal methamphetamine they were "cooking." As we raided their labs, they started varying where they would set up or disguised their labs, trying to prevent us from finding them. But they never got away from the methamphetamine. They just changed their tactics reacting to our actions.

Many violent crimes conducted by street gangs, drug organizations, or family criminal groups are committed across multiple law enforcement jurisdictions. What jurisdiction does the criminal activity that we are investigating fit into for charging subjects? International, federal, state, or local?

Once you have mapped out what criminal activity the targeted criminal enterprise is conducting, you must evaluate what charges are possible. For example, the manufacture of illegal drugs such as methamphetamine violates laws across federal, state, and local jurisdictions. If the criminal activity of your targeted criminal enterprise includes cooking methamphetamine, in what jurisdiction will you bring charges?

In Los Angeles in the 1990s, the FBI investigated most of the bank robberies and brought the cases to the U.S. Attorney's Office. The reason was the federal statute called for longer prison sentences than the State of California. Unless someone was killed and then the State would bring murder charges with the possible death penalty. This situation was negotiated and agreed to by the law enforcement and prosecutors across jurisdictions at the time.

Conversely, at the time I had friends in the FBI in New Orleans that never charged bank robbery federally because the State of Louisiana carried higher prison sentences for bank robberies. They had also agreed to the situation through negotiations with their fellow law enforcement officers and prosecutors. The locals were getting 99-year sentences for their bank robbers prosecuted locally. We called it "getting the most bang for the buck."

This is an area that must be explored and standardized by task force operations. But not set in stone, there will be exceptions to the rule. Develop guidelines with awareness that each situation may be different. Official charging of subjects must take a strategic as well as a tactical overview.

Factors include but are not limited to the following questions: What is the appropriate charge to ask the AUSA or district attorney to levy based upon the subjects placement in the organization? Are you looking for a cooperating witness in the charged subject? Or are they part of the dismantlement phase of the investigation?

The investigation and intelligence collection you have completed by the time you have defined the criminal enterprise, identified the crime problem, and developed an organizational chart will most likely include the specific criminal activity that the targeted criminal enterprise is conducting as their foundation.

The next steps are to identify and research statutes relating to this criminal activity at the various jurisdictional levels. For example, in the NLR investigation our subjects had an affinity for violence. They would often obtain firearms to carry out various crimes. Since many of the NLR members we were investigating had lengthy criminal records, including violent felonies, they were prohibited by federal law from possessing a firearm.

Prior to the formation of the NLR Task Force, an NLR member who was on parole and caught possessing a firearm, was sent back to prison on a parole violation. The general penalty was parole revocation for a six-month period.

Seeing an opportunity to make an impact through weapons possession charges, we began utilizing federal charges under the USC Title 18 Section 922 (g). This statute makes it illegal for a convicted felon to possess a firearm. The penalties included a 10-year prison term without parole. Do the math, six months is less than 10 years. The NLR subjects we charged with 922 (g) were shocked when told what they were facing at their arrest. This worked to our advantage.

We used this charge against the NLR effectively. The 10-year sentence convinced some of the subjects to cooperate with our investigation. If they decided not to cooperate, not only would the 922 (g) charge take them off the streets for 10 years, but it also took them out of the State of California and away from their main power base.

This was a simple but effective tool that we discovered and quickly adopted. The NLR members liked firearms. This law provided us an invaluable investigative tool to target illegal firearms possession.

Once you define the mainstay criminal activity of the targeted criminal enterprise, It is important that each prosecutive avenue regarding the criminal activity is explored. Go with the most effective use of the charges—state or federal—and maximize the impact on the charged subject.

Chapter 13 will explore specific federal statutes that may be useful to you and to your task force operations.

So, when you are conducting your initial assessment of the criminal enterprise, define their criminal activity. What are they doing?

Some specific examples of criminal activity to look for includes, but is not limited to, the following: robberies, car jackings, burglaries, drug trafficking, prostitution, bribery, counterfeiting, theft, embezzlement, fraud, dealing in obscene matter, obstruction of justice, slavery, racketeering, gambling, money laundering, commission of murder-for-hire, assaults, battery extortion, illegal narcotic activity, weapon violations, and murder.

Let's end this chapter with another important learning point. Once you identify a criminal activity that is a primary source of income related directly to the targeted criminal enterprise, look to the past. Let's say the targeted criminal enterprise is infamous for robbery of rival drug dealers.

Do your homework! Go back three years and pull all the solved and unsolved robbery police reports for the area where your targeted criminal enterprise is operating. Once the reports are analyzed, you will discover a wealth of information that may be tied directly to your investigation. You may find police reports that identified several subjects of which you were not aware, or persons of interest or witnesses to interview. This investigative avenue also will identify RICO or VICAR predicate acts that can be attributed to the targeted criminal enterprise.

Enter the relevant information into your searchable database. The true value of the new found information may not be apparent immediately. If these robbery charges are tied to the leaders, the charges will become RICO predicate acts.

As the investigation continues, these identified predicate acts tied to the leaders of the targeted criminal enterprise will be the mainstay of the dismantlement phase of the overall investigation.

Remember, the proper gathering, analyzing, evaluating, and exploiting of criminal intelligence is the backbone of any investigation.

13

Identify, Research, and Know Statutes

Owing to variations in laws from state to state, it would be very difficult to demonstrate and discuss the state statutes relating to task force operations in this work. There are just too many differences in laws from state to state.

Consequently, this chapter will concentrate on federal statutes. That is, statutes that are consistent across all states. Still, be aware that enforcement of these statutes varies with each U.S. judicial district and their U.S. Attorney's Office experience. Other factors that may play into federal prosecutions are informal office policies and national politics.

OK, what does that mean? It is simple. Look to New York City. The U.S. Attorney's Office there is very familiar with the RICO statutes. The New York AUSAs are comfortable using it against any criminal enterprise. Then look at Los Angeles. By the 1990s, there had only been three RICO cases against criminal enterprises. The NLR case was the third RICO case made by the U.S. Attorney's Office decades prior to the 1990s.

Each AUSA will be versed in the practices of their perspective U.S. Attorney's Office. The following excerpts from the USC are simple ones. They are listed in a useable format.

The full RICO statute is pages of mind numbing legal jargon. The examples that I will illustrate in this chapter are statutes that I have used in many cases over the years. I am familiar with them enough to break them down into simpler terms.

Through my experience in applying these statutes in the field, I have found that some AUSAs that haven't prosecuted a criminal enterprise may not be familiar with of these statutes. When the good AUSAs are made aware of the value of these statutes in their prosecution, they will study and implement them. The value of an experienced investigator who has dismantled criminal enterprises in the past utilizing these statutes is not lost on the less experienced AUSA. They have to learn too. Hopefully they will take the advice of their investigators.

Let's review and become familiar with some of the more significant statutes. Then let's define the elements of the crimes that constitute what you will have to prove in court.

The goal of this chapter is to know what to prove and how to prove it in court beyond a reasonable doubt is the standard for federal court, beyond a reasonable doubt, so when you are gathering evidence for a crime, ensure the evidence holds to that standard. It is essential the investigators develop the mindset to meet that standard during the course of the investigation.

Regardless of the press reports about law enforcement, we would never want to convict a person of a crime that they did not commit. It doesn't matter what their criminal background is or what they have done in the past, the law enforcement investigator must play by the rules. We must hold a higher standard. We must always do the right thing. If you want to truly be one of the "good guys" always be ethical and operate within the law. Never compromise.

Now, onto the laws that you can use. There are a myriad of individual federal and state statutes that stand on their own and can be used to disrupt the activities of the targeted criminal enterprise. Once you know who the subjects of your investigation are and what criminal activity they are committing, do not hesitate to bring specific charges against any of the subjects on an individual basis.

For example, if they are robbing banks, use USC Title 18 Section 2113, the bank robbery statute, to a charge them. If there is criminal activity, there will be either a federal or a state statute that you can use to disrupt the daily operations of the targeted criminal enterprise, mostly by charging lower- and mid-level subjects. The convictions for these individual federal or state offenses may be tied into a RICO case against the leaders of the organization in the dismantlement phase of the investigation.

In addition, using federal charges against the mid- and lower-level subjects may lead to the development of a significant informant base.

OK, as in the example in Chapter 12, the NLR liked to get guns and they had felony convictions. We used Title 18 USC 922 (g) to effectively target their criminal activity.

Personally, I like this statute. It provides some real power to our disruption technique. The following is an excerpt from the USC. So take a few minutes and read through the 922 (g) and pull out what you think you have to prove through your investigation of one of your subjects who is caught with a firearm.

18 USC 922: Unlawful acts

From Title 18—CRIMES AND CRIMINAL PROCEDURE
PART I—CRIMES
CHAPTER 44—FIREARMS
(g) It shall be unlawful for any person—

(1) Who has been convicted in any court of, a crime punishable by imprisonment for a term exceeding one year;
(2) Who is a fugitive from justice;
(3) Who is an unlawful user of or addicted to any controlled substance (as defined in section 102 of the Controlled Substances Act (21 U.S.C. 802));
(4) Who has been adjudicated as a mental defective or who has been committed to a mental institution;
(5) Who, being an alien-
   (A) Is illegally or unlawfully in the United States; or
   (B) Except as provided in subsection (y)(2), has been admitted to the United States under a nonimmigrant visa (as that term is defined in section 101 (a)(26) of the Immigration and
Nationality Act (8 U.S.C. 1101(a)(26)));
(6) Who has been discharged from the Armed Forces under dishonorable conditions;
(7) Who, having been a citizen of the United States, has renounced his citizenship;
(8) Who is subject to a court order that-
   (A) Was issued after a hearing of which such person received actual notice, and at which such person had an opportunity to participate;
   (B) Restrains such person from harassing, stalking, or threatening an intimate partner of such person or child of such intimate partner or person,

Or engaging in other conduct that would place an intimate partner in reasonable fear of bodily injury to the partner or child; and

(C) (i) Includes a finding that such person represents a credible threat to the physical safety of such intimate partner or child; or

(ii) by its terms explicitly prohibits the use, attempted use, or threatened use of physical force against such intimate partner or child that would reasonably be expected to cause bodily injury; or

(9) Who has been convicted in any court of a misdemeanor crime of domestic violence,

To ship or transport in interstate or foreign commerce, or possess in or affecting commerce, any firearm or ammunition; or to receive any firearm or ammunition which has been shipped or transported in interstate or foreign commerce.

The next step is to break 922 (g) down and run through some scenarios to make sure you understand how you can use this statute in your investigations. I was taught this was called knowing "the elements of the crime." I learned through experience that if you know the elements of the crime, you will gather evidence to those standards while you are conducting the investigation. The fresher the evidence the stronger the case.

Too many times people unfamiliar with the elements of the crime have to recreate where they saw a piece of critical of evidence. Or they will have to reinterview a key witness months or even years after the crime was committed to meet the elements of the crime for indictment. The best case scenario is to gather the critical piece of evidence or interview the key witness to the elements of the crime as the investigation unfolds. Know the elements of the crime. Investigate to obtaining evidence to prove them and you will build a strong case that will hold up in any court proceeding.

So let's look at 922 (g). First of all there has to be a firearm. The firearm has to be proven to be in the possession of the subject that you are investigating.

That sounds pretty easy but the evidence has to meet the burden of proof, beyond a reasonable doubt. That means that the word of an informant that a subject owns a gun recovered in the informant's house where 20 people besides the subject was arrested, isn't enough proof.

Evidence beyond a reasonable doubt entails evidence akin to the following: The subject's fingerprints are recovered on the firearm, and/or three other witnesses can testify how they know the gun is the subject's and/or the subject confesses the firearm was his at the time of his arrest.

The firearm must also meet some standards are articulated in the 922 (g) statute. The firearm should be examined by the ATF. They will examine it and must show it to be functioning. The ATF will also have to demonstrate the firearm was transported in or affected interstate commerce.

The ATF has been doing this for years. They are usually more than willing to assist. If you are new to the U.S. Judicial District, ask the AUSA for an ATF Agent contact.

So, now you have a functioning firearm that was recovered in your state (outside of Connecticut) and was manufactured in New Haven, Connecticut, covering the interstate aspect.

Let's take a moment to examine your subject. He has to have some type of prior criminal or illegal status to be charged with 922 (g).

Has he been convicted in any court of, a crime punishable by imprisonment for a term exceeding 1 year or convicted in any court of a misdemeanor crime of domestic violence? Was he the subject of a court restraining order? Does the order meet the circumstances as delineated above in 922 (g)? When arrested with the gun, was he a fugitive with active warrants? Can you prove he was an unlawful user of or addicted to any controlled substance? Was he an illegal alien? Was he dishonorably discharged from the U.S. Armed Forces? Was he a U.S. citizen that renounced his citizenship?

If you have any of those circumstances, the subject is eligible to be prosecuted under 922 (g). What we used to call ex-felon in possession of a firearm.

The elements of the crime in 922 (g), ex-felon in possession of a firearm that you have to investigate and gather evidence to show in court, are as follows:

1. The firearm was proven to be in the possession of the subject
2. The firearm was functioning as a firearm
3. The firearm traveled in of affected interstate commerce
4. The subject was a felon, fugitive or had at least one of the criminal prerequisites delineated in the 922 (g) wording
5. You can prove the criminal prerequisite in a court of law beyond a reasonable doubt

It may be helpful to run through a few scenarios. Let's determine whether the subjects can be successfully charged and eventually convicted of violation of 922 (g).

For purposes of this drill let's say the ATF has proven the firearms are functional and have affected or been shipped in interstate commerce.

SCENARIO

You and your task force are stationed in Seattle, Washington; you are investigating an MDTO that has been trafficking cocaine and heroin in the Seattle area. They have been solidifying their position in Washington for the past two years.

Recently, you have been searching for Jose Badillo. He is wanted for the murder of an entire family in Tacoma, Washington. Badillo is a major enforcer of the MDTO. The murder charge is weak, as Badillo called the "hit" but didn't participate. Nonetheless, in the past, Badillo has been convicted of assault with deadly weapon and served two years in a prison in California. He is also an illegal alien who was deported after his prison sentence.

An informant's tip leads your task force to Badillo. He surrenders peacefully when surrounded by 10 task force officers. When arrested, he has a fully loaded .45 cal semiautomatic pistol tucked in his waistband. Badillo is read his *Miranda* rights and admits ownership of the pistol. It is a beautiful piece of work. The pistol has been customized with ivory handles and silver engraved inlay. Badillo tells you he paid $5000 to have it made. He also says he wants it back when he gets out of jail.

This one is easy. All elements met. Badillo has the gun on him when arrested. This was witnessed by 10 task force officers. He admits it is his gun and brags about it in the interview.

As far as criminal prerequisites, Badillo has served over a year incarceration in prison. He is a fugitive from justice. He is an illegal alien. This case could be easily charged under the 922 (g) statute. The value of this charge as a back up to the murder charge is invaluable. Since Badillo is the major enforcer for the MDTO, he would be an excellent cooperating witness, if he could be convinced to cooperate.

However, the 922 (g) charge carries a 10-year sentence and will ensure Badillo is in federal custody for quite some time. If he doesn't cooperate at least he will be out of the picture. As an investigative point, make sure Badillo isn't the main subject of your MDTO before you offer any deals on any charges.

SCENARIO

One more scenario before we move on. Let's say you and your Seattle-based task force are investigating an infamous street gang from Los Angeles, the 48th Street Piru Bloods. They have been moving north in the past decade and have been making themselves know in the past year with some extremely violent acts in the area.

One of their leaders is a suave young man named Jaris Reginald Washington, who goes by the street name of T Bone.

T Bone is a U.S. citizen, and never convicted of a felony, but he has been convicted of a misdemeanor for domestic violence. Informant information is that T Bone and several Bloods are in a Motel 6 in Tacoma. They are armed to the teeth with firearms.

You, the ATF, and the task force respond to the Motel 6. You find T Bone and three other Blood members in the hotel room.

However, there is only one firearm found in the hotel room. It is tucked in between the mattress. It is a .40 cal Glock Model 22 semiautomatic pistol. It was reportedly stolen in Portland, Oregon.

No one who is arrested makes any statements. All of them request attorneys. The room is registered to a female named Teresa Johnson with a fictitious address; no leads there. The ATF processes the firearm. No finger prints or DNA is found.

This is hard one on investigators. You have a stolen gun in a room with four of the major players of your task force investigation, including the leader T Bone. But based upon the evidence that I presented to you, you can't charge anyone with the 922 (g).

T Bone has a conviction for domestic violence. If he was found to have possession of the firearm, he could be charged; however, he cannot be charged with the current information. You can't prove that T Bone possessed the firearm. However, make sure the gun, evidence, and everything is preserved for future use.

If any of the three other subjects is arrested for any future criminal activity, they may end up cooperating. Eventually, they may provide evidence that T Bone or another was in possession of that particular Glock pistol. Besides, there might be a homicide or shooting that ballistic evidence may match the Glock, which hasn't been uncovered yet.

Hopefully this section has helped you understand the 922 (g) statute and its uses when targeting a criminal enterprise that uses guns to commit their crimes or protect their illegal assets.

The next statute is also related to firearms. As its title states, it basically relates to using a firearm in commission of another crime.

18 USC 924: Use of a firearm in commission of a crime

From Title 18—CRIMES AND CRIMINAL PROCEDURE
PART I—CRIMES
CHAPTER 44—FIREARMS
§924. Penalties

(c)(1)(A) Except to the extent that a greater minimum sentence is otherwise provided by this subsection or by any other provision of law, any person who, during and in relation to any crime of violence or drug trafficking crime (including a crime of violence or drug trafficking crime that provides for an enhanced punishment if committed by the use of a deadly or dangerous weapon or device) for which the person may be prosecuted in a court of the United States, uses or carries a firearm, or who, in furtherance of any such crime, possesses a firearm, shall, in addition to the punishment provided for such crime of violence or drug trafficking crime-
  (i)   Be sentenced to a term of imprisonment of not less than 5 years;
  (ii) if the firearm is brandished, be sentenced to a term of imprisonment of not less than 7 years; and
  (iii) if the firearm is discharged, be sentenced to a term of imprisonment of not less than 10 years
(B) If the firearm possessed by a person convicted of a violation of this subsection-
  (i)   Is a short-barreled rifle, short-barreled shotgun, or semiautomatic assault weapon, the person shall be sentenced to a term of imprisonment of not less than 10 years; or
  (ii) is a machinegun or a destructive device, or is equipped with a firearm silencer or firearm muffler, the person shall be sentenced to a term of imprisonment of not less than 30 years
(C) In the case of a second or subsequent conviction under this subsection, the person shall—
  (i)   Be sentenced to a term of imprisonment of not less than 25 years; and
  (ii) if the firearm involved is a machinegun or a destructive device, or is equipped with a firearm silencer or firearm muffler, be sentenced to imprisonment for life

(D) Notwithstanding any other provision of law—
  (i) a Court shall not place on probation any person convicted of a violation of this subsection; and
  (ii) no term of imprisonment imposed on a person under this subsection shall run concurrently with any other term of imprisonment imposed on the person, including any term of imprisonment imposed for the crime of violence or drug trafficking crime during which the firearm was used, carried, or possessed
(2) For purposes of this subsection, the term "drug trafficking crime" means any felony punishable under the Controlled Substances Act (21 U.S.C. 801 et seq.), the Controlled Substances Import and Export Act (21 U.S.C. 951 et seq.), or Chapter 705 of Title 46
(3) For purposes of this subsection the term "crime of violence" means an offense that is a felony and—
  (A) Has as an element the use, attempted use, or threatened use of physical force against the person or property of another, or
  (B) That by its nature, involves a substantial risk that physical force against the person or property of another may be used in the course of committing the offense
(4) For purposes of this subsection, the term "brandish" means, with respect to a firearm, to display all or part of the firearm, or otherwise make the presence of the firearm known to another person, in order to intimidate that person, regardless of whether the firearm is directly visible to that person
(5) Except to the extent that a greater minimum sentence is otherwise provided under this subsection, or by any other provision of law, any person who, during and in relation to any crime of violence or drug trafficking crime (including a crime of violence or drug trafficking crime that provides for an enhanced punishment if committed by the use of a deadly or dangerous weapon or device) for which the person may be prosecuted in a court of the United States, uses or carries armor piercing ammunition, or who, in furtherance of any such crime, possesses armor piercing ammunition, shall, in addition to the punishment provided for such crime of violence or drug trafficking crime or conviction under this section—
  (A) Be sentenced to a term of imprisonment of not less than 15 years; and
  (B) If death results from the use of such ammunition—

(i) If the killing is murder (as defined in Section 1111), be punished by death or sentenced to a term of imprisonment for any term of years or for life; and

(ii) if the killing is manslaughter (as defined in Section 1112), be punished as provided in Section 1112

This statute, Title 18 924 (c), is extremely important to any investigator targeting criminal enterprises.

This statute provides enhancements to sentencing if the subject used a firearm in commission of a federal crime. This statute can be applied to any federal crime that involves violence or drug trafficking activity.

Some of the penalties are substantial, with sections calling for the death penalty in certain circumstances. The penalties under this statute are in addition to any sentences that are imposed for the initial federal crimes. They are very effective in any plea bargaining with potential witnesses or informants.

The elements of the crime of using a firearm are as follows:

1. Prove the subject used a firearm in commission of the crime.
2. Prove the crime was a violent felony and/or a drug trafficking crime.
3. Prove the firearm was operational at the time of the offense.
4. Prove the subject committed the offense beyond a reasonable doubt in federal court.

The 924 (c) statute is extremely useful. It can be applied where any violent crime or drug-related crime is committed and a firearm was involved. Some of the cases I investigated and applied the 924 (c) statute included bank robbery, kidnapping, extortion, gangs, MDTOs, and car jackings.

The sentences can be increased significantly with these firearms enhancements. The 924 (c) statute can be useful in the disruption and dismantlement phases of your criminal enterprise investigations. The statute is also a useful bargaining tool in the conversion of subject to cooperating witness.

If the criminal enterprise you are investigating is involved in violent crimes, they will undoubtedly use firearms in the course of their criminal activity. The enhancements for using firearms in commission of a crime vary from five years to the death penalty depending on the circumstances of the case. These charges are above and beyond the base charge. The charges for use of a firearm in commission of a crime will add substantial time to the defendant's prison time at sentencing.

For example, as we saw in Los Angeles in the 1990s, the Rollin 60s Crips were arming your recruits and having them rob banks for gang membership. If your criminal enterprise is using bank robbery as a recruit-ment tool and arming the robbers, the basic federal bank robbery statute Title 18 2113 (a) (d) for armed bank robbery would be the base charge. But if the robbers had firearms recovered in the investigation, even if they didn't show them, the Title 18 924 (c) use of a firearm in commission of a crime with a five-year penalty would also be levied, in addition to the bank rob-bery charge. If they brandished the firearm a seven-year 924 (c) charge would be added. If they fired the weapon, the prison term increases to 10 years. Since the 924 (c) sentencing terms are substantial, the bargaining for a plea deal often includes the subject pleading to the base charges if the AUSA drops the 924 (c) charges. As mentioned before, this can be an excel-lent bargaining tool when searching for cooperating witnesses to testify against the criminal enterprise.

Although the 924 (c) charges cannot be used as RICO predicate acts themselves, the base charges of robbery, murder, assault, and many other crimes where firearms are used qualify as RICO predicate acts.

SCENARIO

So, scenario time. A bank robber walks into a bank in your territory. He pulls down his ski mask and brandishes a black colored semiautomatic pistol. He orders everyone on the ground and threatens customers and bank employees with the black pistol. He demands money and throws a white cloth pillowcase to a male teller. The bank employees scram-ble to gather money from the teller's drawers. They empty the cash drawers and throw the money-laden pillowcase to the robber. He picks up the loot and backs out of the bank door, pointing the pistol at the peo-ple laying on the bank floor. He yells, "First one out the door gets shot."

The bank robber runs through the bank parking lot and jumps over a block wall fence. Unknown to the robber, the tellers included two dye packs with the loot in the pillowcase. Just as he reaches his getaway car, the dye packs explode. The money in the pillowcase is stained with red dye and CS gas spews into the car. The bank robber is stunned. A police car pulls into the alley and the bank robbery is quickly taken into custody. The money is recovered and taken into evidence. The ski mask and black pistol are also recovered by the arresting officer. The bank robber turns out to be a juvenile. He is just 17 years old. He confesses to interviewing officers. He tells them that he robbed the bank as part of a gang initiation.

The police call your task force, as they have an officer as a full-time member. The bank robber is trying to gain membership to the 34th Forest Street Crips, the main target of your gang Task Force. His information is valuable. He was recruited by one of your main subjects, Tyrone Duggan. Tyrone is a leader of the 34th Forest Street Crips. With the juvenile testifying against Tyrone, you believe Tyrone could be charged with the bank robbery as a RICO predicate act. The AUSA agrees.

Because he is a juvenile, the AUSA must obtain special Department of Justice (DOJ) permission to charge the bank robber in federal court. The AUSA understands the value of the bank robber's testimony and cooperation. He obtains the DOJ permission and charges the juvenile with the bank robbery. He asks about the black pistol use in the bank robbery. You found out the black pistol was an airsoft pistol, not a firearm. Based upon the elements of the crime, can you bring a 924 (c) charge on the juvenile?

The answer is no, you cannot consider the 924 (c) charge. The elements call for a firearm that is functional. The airsoft gun would not qualify as a firearm. The AUSA will have to charge the juvenile with Title 18 Section 2113 (a) (d) bank robbery. It would still qualify as a RICO predicate act on Tyrone in your Crip Task Force case.

The next statute we will examine is the violent crimes in aid of racketeering activity or VICAR statute. It can be very useful in the disruption and dismantlement of the targeted criminal enterprise.

18 U.S. Code § 1959—Violent Crimes in Aid of Racketeering Activity

(a) Whoever, as consideration for the receipt of, or as consideration for a promise or agreement to pay, anything of pecuniary value from an enterprise engaged in racketeering activity, or for the purpose of gaining entrance to or maintaining or increasing position in an enterprise engaged in racketeering activity, murders, kidnaps, maims, assaults with a dangerous weapon, commits assault resulting in serious bodily injury upon, or threatens to commit a crime of violence against any individual in violation of the laws of any State or the United States, or attempts or conspires so to do, shall be punished—

    (1) For murder, by death or life imprisonment, or a fine under this title, or both; and for kidnapping, by imprisonment for any term of years or for life, or a fine under this title, or both;

    (2) For maiming, by imprisonment for not more than thirty years or a fine under this title, or both;

(3) For assault with a dangerous weapon or assault resulting in serious bodily injury, by imprisonment for not more than twenty years or a fine under this title, or both;

(4) For threatening to commit a crime of violence, by imprisonment for not more than five years or a fine under this title, or both;

(5) For attempting or conspiring to commit murder or kidnapping, by imprisonment for not more than ten years or a fine under this title, or both; and

(6) For attempting or conspiring to commit a crime involving maiming, assault with a dangerous weapon, or assault resulting in serious bodily injury, by imprisonment for not more than three years or a fine of [1] under this title, or both

(b) As used in this section—

(1) "Racketeering activity" has the meaning set forth in section 1961 of this title; and

(2) "Enterprise" includes any partnership, corporation, association, or other legal entity, and any union or group of individuals associated in fact although not a legal entity, which is engaged in, or the activities of which affect, interstate or foreign commerce

Although there are similarities between VICAR and RICO, there are different uses for each of the statutes.

The RICO statute is used to dismantle the entire criminal enterprise by using two predicate acts against each of the subjects targeted by the investigation.

The VICAR statute uses specific violent crimes charges against individuals who commit these violent crimes for an enterprise. The VICAR charge can stand by itself and a subject can be charged with the one count. For example, a murder done for a gang can be charged under VICAR, no need for additional predicate acts. However, the VICAR conviction can be also used as a predicate act under the RICO statute.

Confused? Don't be; it is rather simple. Let's lay it out in a scenario and clear things up.

SCENARIO

Your federal task force is targeting the Insane Loco Lamos (ILL), a violent drug dealing street gang that has been raping, robbing, and killing people in your jurisdiction for the past two years. In the beginning stages of the investigation, you uncover strong evidence in an unsolved homicide of a police informant. The informant was killed by Paulo Rameriz, an ILL member.

Juanita Rameriz, Paulo's ex-wife is looking for revenge on him for dumping her for a younger woman. She has come to the task force with a bushel full of evidence. She brings you the 9 mm Beretta used to kill the informant. The serial number verifies it is a stolen gun. The ballistics tests match up on seven of the ten slugs taken out of the informant. Paulo's fingerprints are on the gun. She also brings a letter from Jose Evilano. Evilano is the leader of the ILL. In the letter, Evilano writes congratulations to Paulo on the "hit on the rat at the grocery store." The informant was killed in the local Safeway grocery store parking lot. Evilano continues to praise Paulo in his letter. He promotes Paulo to boss because of the homicide. Throughout the letter Evilano praises Paulo's commitment to the ILL.

The icing on the cake is that two witnesses to the homicide pick Paulo out of a photo lineup as the shooter.

Presented with overwhelming evidence, the AUSA agrees to charge Paulo with VICAR for the murder of the informant.

The task force reasons that the ILL will be disrupted by the removal of Paulo from the gang, as Paulo had assumed the role of enforcer for the ILL. A strategic move to disrupt the ILL and after the VICAR conviction have a readymade RICO predicate act on both Paulo Rameriz and Jose Evilano.

Since the crime was committed for the enterprise as evidenced by the letter from Jose Evilano and was a crime of violence as delineated under VICAR USC Section 1959, Paulo can be charged under the VICAR statute.

Once convicted of the VICAR murder done for the ILL, both ILL leaders, Jose and Paulo, can be charged with the murder as a RICO predicate act. Does that clear things up somewhat?

So, the elements of the VICAR statute that you will have to prove are as follows:

1. The offense must be an act of violence as articulated under USC Title 18 Section 1959 (a) (1–6) (see statute wording above).
2. Prove the enterprise. (Evidence gathered to prove the enterprise can be used in again in future RICO charges.)
3. Prove the offense was committed for the benefit of the enterprise.
4. Prove the subject committed the offense beyond a reasonable doubt in federal court.

We used the VICAR statute effectively against the NLR. We utilized VICAR in the NLR affinity for violent crime. The NLR committed murder, assault, robbery, extortion, and hate crimes.

In one example, we charged a subject named "Hoss" with assault VICAR with serious bodily injury and attempted murder involving the robbery of a drug dealer who had been dealing methamphetamine to the NLR. Hoss attacked and beat the drug dealer with a Maglite, causing serve head injury and putting him in the hospital. Hoss robbed him, taking his money and drugs.

Hoss was convicted of the VICAR for this assault. Later, when we were building a RICO case on the NLR, we utilized this VICAR conviction as a RICO predicate act on another NLR leader "Snake." That snake had condoned the assault on the drug dealer for not paying taxes to the NLR for dealing methamphetamine in their territory. Snake was charged with this attempted murder and several other offenses, including murder in the overall RICO case.

In fact, one of the initial NLR cases led to the indictment of two NLR members with violation of the VICAR statute. The charges stemmed from the hate crime slashing (attempted murder) of a black inmate at the West Valley Detention Center.

The VICAR charge is a good tool in itself but is also a precursor to the RICO charges. The VICAR statute assists the investigation by allowing significant charges against leaders and principals of the targeted criminal enterprise. VICAR is a valuable disruption tool available to criminal investigators.

Since VICAR charges can be enfolded into the future RICO cases, it is a worthy investment and will play well into the dismantlement phase of the criminal investigation into the targeted criminal enterprise.

Early VICAR charges also allow prosecutors to test the proof gathered regarding the "enterprise" in federal court. Since you have to prove the target is an enterprise in both the VICAR and RICO statutes under the same burden of proof, once proven in federal court in a VICAR case, it will hold up in future RICO prosecutions.

Attorneys love precedent set in Federal Court. So once they prove the criminal enterprise in the VICAR case, the same evidence will be presented in the RICO case at a high level of confidence by the AUSA.

The next federal statute that we will examine with be out of USC Section 18 and into USC Section 21. The drug statutes are very valuable if the targeted criminal enterprise is a drug organization or their criminal activity includes the trafficking of illegal narcotics. With so much easy money to be made in the illegal drug trade, most criminal enterprises have some nexus to drugs.

We will start with simple possession. We will then move to distribution and then finally to the continuing criminal enterprise (CCE) charges. The CCE charges were specifically written to dismantle drug-fueled criminal enterprises.

Title 21 USC 841: Prohibited acts A

From Title 21—FOOD AND DRUGS
CHAPTER 13—DRUG ABUSE PREVENTION AND CONTROL
SUBCHAPTER I—CONTROL AND ENFORCEMENT
Part D—Offenses and Penalties
§841. Prohibited acts A

(a) Unlawful acts
   Except as authorized by this subchapter, it shall be unlawful for any person knowingly or intentionally-
   (1) To manufacture, distribute, or dispense, or possess with intent to manufacture, distribute, or dispense, a controlled substance; or
   (2) To create, distribute, or dispense, or possess with intent to distribute or dispense, a counterfeit substance

The above excerpt is from the federal drug statutes under Title 21 of the USC. There is additional information available on the website for the USC.

I wanted to pull the gist of the federal drug laws, which makes it illegal to manufacture, distribute, and possess a controlled substance. The definitions of controlled substance are outlined at length in the USC.

The point of this section is to emphasize that if your targeted criminal enterprise is involved in illegal drug trafficking, there are federal statutes that will greatly assist you in their disruption and dismantlement.

As mentioned earlier in the initial formation of the task force, if the targeted criminal enterprise is involved in significant international drug trafficking, the DEA may choose to join the task force.

However, if the amounts are not significant, the DEA may only be available to the Task Force on an advisory basis. The FBI is capable of investigating Title 21 violations but the DEA agents are experts at these statutes. I would recommend seeking their advice when investigating Title 21 violations. Just watch so they don't steal your cases and informants!

OK, the first example that we reviewed made it illegal for some people to possess firearms if they met certain conditions, that is, they were convicted felons.

Under Title 21 USC 841, it is illegal for people to manufacture, distribute, or dispense, or possess with intent to manufacture, distribute, or dispense a controlled substance; or to create, distribute, or dispense, or possess with intent to distribute or dispense a counterfeit substance.

Just having (possessing) a controlled substance (illegal narcotics) is against the law. The manufacturing and distribution elements are the basis for any drug-related criminal enterprise.

The elements of the crime of drug possession are as follows:

1. Prove the subject possessed the illegal substance.
2. Prove an interstate nexus.
3. Prove the subject committed the offense beyond a reasonable doubt in federal court.

As in the firearms in possession of a firearm violation, the key to illegal narcotics investigations is proving possession.

Narcotics investigations require hours of surveillance and background work. Many of the criminal enterprise investigative techniques are vital to dismantlement of an illegal narcotics trafficking organization. Define the enterprise, identify the leaders, disrupt their daily operations, and dismantle the organization.

Couple of difficulties with narcotics investigations. Since there is a lot of money to be made in drug trafficking, there will always be people who will take the risk of being caught and imprisoned. As soon as you arrest one person, another with take his or her place, same with organizations. From the time you dismantle an organization, another group is moving dope in the same area.

As long as there is a demand for the product and the general public is willing to pay the going price, there will be illegal drug trafficking. So as soon as you dismantle one trafficking group, there will be another to take its place.

The other major obstacle to investigating a major drug trafficking criminal enterprise is the most worthy targets of the investigation are generally not in the United States and are difficult, or impossible to arrest, detain, or truly disrupt their operations.

For example, Joaquin "El Chapo" Guzman has been one of the biggest drug dealers in the world for years. In 2015, at the time I was writing this book, he just had escaped from the maximum security prison in

Mexico, where he was serving time for drug trafficking. The last time he escaped from a Mexican prison, he was on the run for 13 years. Until the day he dies, Guzman will continue to run a worldwide narcotics trafficking criminal enterprise.

With all that being said, I am not advocating throwing up your hands and giving up on any worthwhile investigations.

In 1994, I investigated a cell of the Guzman organization. We indicted 10 people, convicted nine (one was in Mexico and was not brought to the United States for trial) and seized over one and a half tons of cocaine.

The cell was using tractor trailer rigs to transport cocaine from El Paso, Texas, to Los Angeles. They were using tunnels cut through the earth under the Juarez River, which borders the cities of El Paso, Texas, and Juarez, Mexico.

The case was tied to Guzman through intelligence, but there was nothing solid enough that we could use in court to indict him. It was a worthwhile case and I gained vast experience through the effort.

A major investigative avenue in the investigation of illegal narcotics criminal enterprises is the identification of the leaders or international organizations that the regional enterprises are affiliated.

Informant information, always important in any organized crime investigation, takes on a vital role in narcotics investigations. The higher placed the informant is in the organization, the more likely the investigation will truly disrupt the criminal enterprises effectiveness.

However, be aware that many of these international drug trafficking organizations have hierarchies that are based upon family and penetrating those is extremely difficult.

There is also an aspect to these organizations that is extremely violent; some of the worst violence acts committed were done by these people to former informants, their families, and even their entire villages.

Back to the matter at hand, the investigation of the narcotics criminal enterprise depends on finding the dope and proving whose dope it was when it was seized.

Title 21 USC 844 is the statute that can be used to charge narcotics possession in federal court.

Be aware that each judicial district has prosecutive guidelines that set the threshold for cases that will be prosecuted in their districts. Sometimes, the prosecutive guidelines are way outside the minimum needed to prosecute a case in federal court. For example, in Los Angeles in the 1990s, the threshold was five kilograms of cocaine. So, if you recovered four kilograms of cocaine, they wouldn't prosecute the case through the federal system. Investigating cases in that environment was very difficult; it was downright maddening.

Again, I would emphasize the need to have a formalized OCDETF with an assigned AUSA who can make the case to prosecute cases under the guidelines.

The next following two excerpts of the USC deals with penalties and forfeitures under Title 21.

21 USC 844: Penalties for simple possession

From Title 21—FOOD AND DRUGS
CHAPTER 13—DRUG ABUSE PREVENTION AND CONTROL
SUBCHAPTER I—CONTROL AND ENFORCEMENT
Part D—Offenses and Penalties
§844. Penalties for simple possession

(a) Unlawful acts; penalties

It shall be unlawful for any person knowingly or intentionally to possess a controlled substance unless such substance was obtained directly, or pursuant to a valid prescription or order, from a practitioner, while acting in the course of his professional practice, or except as otherwise authorized by this subchapter or subchapter II of this chapter. It shall be unlawful for any person knowingly or intentionally to possess any list I chemical obtained pursuant to or under authority of a registration issued to that person under section 823 of this title or section 958 of this title if that registration has been revoked or suspended, if that registration has expired, or if the registrant has ceased to do business in the manner contemplated by his registration. It shall be unlawful for any person to knowingly or intentionally purchase at retail during a 30-day period more than 9 grams of ephedrine base, pseudoephedrine base, or phenylpropanolamine base in a scheduled listed chemical product, except that, of such 9 grams, not more than 7.5 grams may be imported by means of shipping through any private or commercial carrier or the Postal Service. Any person who violates this subsection may be sentenced to a term of imprisonment of not more than 1 year, and shall be fined a minimum of $1,000, or both, except that if he commits such offense after a prior conviction under this subchapter or subchapter II of this chapter, or a prior conviction for any drug, narcotic, or chemical offense chargeable under the law of any State, has become final, he shall be sentenced to a term of imprisonment for not less than 15 days but not more than 2 years, and shall be fined a minimum of $2,500, except, further, that if he commits such offense after two or more prior convictions under this subchapter or subchapter II of this chapter, or two or more prior convictions for any drug, narcotic, or chemical offense chargeable under the law of any State, or a combination of two or more such offenses have become final, he shall be sentenced to a term of imprisonment for not less than 90 days but not more than 3 years, and shall be fined a minimum of $5,000. Notwithstanding any penalty provided in this subsection, any person convicted under this subsection for the possession of flunitrazepam shall be imprisoned for not more than 3 years, shall be fined as otherwise provided in this section, or both. The imposition or execution of a minimum sentence required to be imposed under this subsection shall not be suspended or deferred. Further, upon conviction, a person who violates this subsection shall be fined the reasonable costs of the investigation and prosecution of the offense, including the costs of prosecution of an offense as defined in sections 1918 and 1920 of title 28, except that this sentence shall not apply and a fine under this section need not be imposed if the court determines under the provision of title 18 that the defendant lacks the ability to pay.

The penalty section stands on its own. Bear in mind there are prosecutive guidelines that had been written that was meant to standardize the sentencing in all federal cases. However, the guidelines that were written were only taken under advisement of federal judges, which means judges could sentence subjects at their discretion in spite of the federal guidelines.

I would highly recommend once you identify a charge that you think you will be exploring on a subject of your investigation, pull the statutes, and do your homework. Make sure you discuss it with your AUSA. Discussions should include the practices of the local judicial district and the sentencing habits of the local judges. Once this homework is done on a charge, you will be more likely to succeed in your investigations and subsequent prosecutions. Once you have been through the system and utilized any statute to charge a subject, you will be versed in these charges. This experience will be instrumental when investigating other subjects and criminal enterprises.

21 USC 853: Criminal forfeitures

From Title 21—FOOD AND DRUGS
CHAPTER 13—DRUG ABUSE PREVENTION AND CONTROL
SUBCHAPTER I—CONTROL AND ENFORCEMENT
Part D—Offenses and Penalties
§853. Criminal forfeitures

(a) Property subject to criminal forfeiture

Any person convicted of a violation of this subchapter or subchapter II of this chapter punishable by imprisonment for more than one year shall forfeit to the United States, irrespective of any provision of State law—

(1) Any property constituting, or derived from, any proceeds the person obtained, directly or indirectly, as the result of such violation;

(2) Any of the person's property used, or intended to be used, in any manner or part, to commit, or to facilitate the commission of, such violation; and

(3) In the case of a person convicted of engaging in a continuing criminal enterprise in violation of section 848 of this title, the person shall forfeit, in addition to any property described in paragraph (1) or (2), any of his interest in, claims against, and property or contractual rights affording a source of control over, the continuing criminal enterprise.

The court, in imposing sentence on such person, shall order, in addition to any other sentence imposed pursuant to this subchapter or subchapter II of this chapter, that the person forfeit to the United States all property described in this subsection. In lieu of a fine otherwise authorized by this part, a defendant who derives profits or other proceeds from an offense may be fined not more than twice the gross profits or other proceeds.

Next to the RICO statute, forfeiture laws are some of the most valuable tools available to a task force investigating a criminal enterprise.

Remember that committing crimes for financial gain is the livelihood of any criminal. Making money is the goal of the criminal enterprise. If a criminal enterprise is not financially stable, it cannot function.

Paying their operatives on a daily basis is the cornerstone of a successful criminal enterprise. The leaders of the criminal enterprise receive a bulk of profits collected from the criminal activity. The leaders will invest cash, buy property, vehicles, and other expensive items with the profits from their illegal business. They will view their financial gains as the privilege of their rank in the criminal enterprise.

Think about taking the material things gathered because of their illegal activity and how very damaging it is to have that financial lifeline cut, especially to the individual leaders of the criminal enterprise. They spend the majority of their time trying to make money and protect their profits from the cops and rival criminals.

As a criminal king pin, to be sitting in jail facing RICO charges and having your family in trouble because the feds are seizing your house, cars, and money is to say the least, distressing.

In addition, the seizure of large amounts of cash or bank accounts during the investigation can and will disrupt the daily operations of the targeted criminal enterprise. There is nothing more damaging to a criminal enterprise than not having the ability to pay its bills and pay them on time. The credibility of any organization, criminal or legitimate, depends on the timely payment of debts and collection of income.

The use of seizure statutes in conjunction with the RICO statute in your investigation will disrupt and eventually dismantle the entire criminal enterprise.

The elements of the crime for seizures are as follows:

1. Prove the substantive drug case beyond a reasonable doubt in federal court.
2. Prove the items targeted for seizure were obtained from funds derived from criminal activity.

In the early 1990s when I was investigating MDTOs in Los Angeles, our subjects were buying expensive cars and paying cash for houses. Back then, all law enforcement was having a field day, seizing their assets through these statutes.

Nevertheless, the criminals learn and evolve. Over time they learned to hide their assets. At first they started putting the titles for the houses and cars in their wife's name. But that wasn't that hard for us to figure out and we still took all their property. Then they got smarter and started leasing cars instead of buying them. They would rent houses and send most of their money down to Mexico through Western Union or these small check cashing joints littered about Los Angeles.

The point being the crooks will do everything they can to protect their money. Utilizing the forfeiture laws to target the criminal enterprise is an effective and efficient tool to complete your mission.

Title 21 §848. Continuing criminal enterprise

(a) Penalties; forfeitures

Any person who engages in a continuing criminal enterprise shall be sentenced to a term of imprisonment which may not be less than 20 years and which may be up to life imprisonment, to a fine not to exceed the greater of that authorized in accordance with the provisions of title 18 or $2,000,000 if the defendant is an individual or $5,000,000 if the defendant is other than an individual, and to the forfeiture prescribed in section 853 of this title; except that if any person engages in such activity after one or more prior convictions of him under this section have become final, he shall be sentenced to a term of imprisonment which may not be less than 30 years and which may be up to life imprisonment, to a fine not to exceed the greater of twice the amount authorized in accordance with the provisions of title 18 or $4,000,000 if the defendant is an individual or $10,000,000 if the defendant is other than an individual, and to the forfeiture prescribed in section 853 of this title.

(b) Life imprisonment for engaging in continuing criminal enterprise

Any person who engages in a continuing criminal enterprise shall be imprisoned for life and fined in accordance with subsection (a) of this section, if—

(1) Such person is the principal administrator, organizer, or leader of the enterprise or is one of several such principal administrators, organizers, or leaders; and

(2) (A) The violation referred to in subsection (c)(1) of this section involved at least 300 times the quantity of a substance described in subsection 841 (b)(1)(B) of this title, or

(B) The enterprise, or any other enterprise in which the defendant was the principal or one of several principal administrators, organizers, or leaders, received $10 million dollars in gross receipts during any twelve-month period of its existence for the manufacture, importation, or distribution of a substance described in section 841 (b)(1)(B) of this title

(c) "Continuing criminal enterprise" defined

For purposes of subsection (a) of this section, a person is engaged in a continuing criminal enterprise if—

(1) He violates any provision of this subchapter or subchapter II of this chapter the punishment for which is a felony, and

(2) Such violation is a part of a continuing series of violations of this subchapter or subchapter II of this chapter—

 (A) Which are undertaken by such person in concert with five or more other persons with respect to whom such person occupies a position of organizer, a supervisory position, or any other position of management, and

 (B) From which such person obtains substantial income or resources

(d) Suspension of sentence and probation prohibited

In the case of any sentence imposed under this section, imposition or execution of such sentence shall not be suspended, probation shall not be granted, and the Act of July 15, 1932 (D.C. Code, secs. 24–203-24–207), shall not apply

(e) Death penalty

(1) In addition to the other penalties set forth in this section—

 (A) Any person engaging in or working in furtherance of a continuing criminal enterprise, or any person engaging in an offense punishable under section 841 (b)(1)(A) 1 of this title or section 960 (b)(1) 1 of this title who intentionally kills or counsels, commands, induces, procures, or causes the intentional killing of an individual and such killing results, shall be sentenced to any term of imprisonment, which shall not be less than 20 years, and which may be up to life imprisonment, or may be sentenced to death; and

 (B) Any person, during the commission of, in furtherance of, or while attempting to avoid apprehension, prosecution or service of a prison sentence for, a felony violation of this subchapter or subchapter II of this chapter who intentionally kills or counsels, commands, induces, procures, or causes the intentional killing of any Federal, State, or local law enforcement officer engaged in, or on account of, the performance of such officer's official duties and such killing results, shall be sentenced to any term of imprisonment, which shall not be less than 20 years, and which may be up to life imprisonment, or may be sentenced to death.

(2) As used in paragraph (1)(B), the term "law enforcement officer" means a public servant authorized by law or by a Government agency or Congress to conduct or engage in the prevention, investigation, prosecution or adjudication of an offense, and includes those engaged in corrections, probation, or parole functions.

The CCE statute is an excellent federal statute that carries substantial penalties for the leaders of the criminal enterprise. The CCE statute was conceived for use in the "war on drugs." It was intended to assist in the disruption and dismantlement of major Colombian and Mexican drug trafficking cartels.

Of course, you have to be able to get your hands on these people to charge them with anything. Unfortunately, most of them do not venture into countries or territories that are well policed or extradition friendly with the United States.

Under Title 21, CCE requires the criminal enterprise be related to drugs and the amounts of drugs or money of the organization must be substantial. The statute calls for 300 times the amount of drugs as described in Title 21 Subsection 841 (b)(1)(B), and/or 10 million dollars revenue, in a years' time frame.

The elements of the crime for CCE are as follows:

1. Prove the criminal enterprise, at least five people working in concert.
2. Prove the subject's role was in a position of organizer, a supervisory position, or any other management position, and such person obtains substantial income or resources.
3. Prove the volume of drugs is at least 300 times the amount of drugs as described in Title 21 Subsection 841 (b)(1)(B), and/or 10 million dollars revenue, in a years' time frame.
4. Prove the substantive drug cases beyond a reasonable doubt in federal court.

That is a lot of money and dope. You can see that CCE is for large-scale narcotics trafficking organizations. We couldn't use it on most of the gangs in Los Angeles, because they never reached the level of drug trafficking or financial gain required for the statute. I did explore its use with the AUSA on the NLR case but we didn't meet the requirements for money or drugs.

18 USC 1961: Definitions

From Title 18—CRIMES AND CRIMINAL PROCEDURE
CHAPTER 96—RACKETEER INFLUENCED AND CORRUPT
  ORGANIZATIONS
§1961. Definitions

As used in this chapter—
  (1) "Racketeering activity" means (A) any act or threat involv-
      ing murder, kidnapping, gambling, arson, robbery, bribery,
      extortion, dealing in obscene matter, or dealing in a controlled
      substance or listed chemical (as defined in section 102 of the
      Controlled Substances Act), which is chargeable under State
      law and punishable by imprisonment for more than one year;
      (B) any act which is indictable under any of the following pro-
      visions of title 18, United States Code (see Appendix for spe-
      cific statutes).
  (2) "State" means any State of the United States, the District of
      Columbia, the Commonwealth of Puerto Rico, any territory or
      possession of the United States, any political subdivision, or
      any department, agency, or instrumentality thereof;
  (3) "Person" includes any individual or entity capable of holding
      a legal or beneficial interest in property;
  (4) "Enterprise" includes any individual, partnership, corpora-
      tion, association, or other legal entity, and any union or group
      of individuals associated in fact although not a legal entity;
  (5) "Pattern of racketeering activity" requires at least two acts of
      racketeering activity, one of which occurred after the effective
      date of this chapter and the last of which occurred within ten
      years (excluding any period of imprisonment) after the com-
      mission of a prior act of racketeering activity;
  (6) "Unlawful debt" means a debt (A) incurred or contracted in
      gambling activity which was in violation of the law of the
      United States, a State or political subdivision thereof, or which
      is unenforceable under State or Federal law in whole or in part
      as to principal or interest because of the laws relating to usury,
      and (B) which was incurred in connection with the business of
      gambling in violation of the law of the United States, a State or
      political subdivision thereof, or the business of lending money
      or a thing of value at a rate usurious under State or Federal law,
      where the usurious rate is at least twice the enforceable rate;

(7) "Racketeering investigator" means any attorney or investigator so designated by the Attorney General and charged with the duty of enforcing or carrying into effect this chapter;

(8) "Racketeering investigation" means any inquiry conducted by any racketeering investigator for the purpose of ascertaining whether any person has been involved in any violation of this chapter or of any final order, judgment, or decree of any court of the United States, duly entered in any case or proceeding arising under this chapter;

(9) "Documentary material" includes any book, paper, document, record, recording, or other material; and

(10) "Attorney General" includes the Attorney General of the United States, the Deputy Attorney General of the United States, the Associate Attorney General of the United States, any Assistant Attorney General of the United States, or any employee of the Department of Justice or any employee of any department or agency of the United States so designated by the Attorney General to carry out the powers conferred on the Attorney General by this chapter. Any department or agency so designated may use in investigations authorized by this chapter either the investigative provisions of this chapter or the investigative power of such department or agency otherwise conferred by law.

The RICO statute has been successfully utilized by many prosecutors and investigators to dismantle criminal enterprises since the 1970s.

The FBI and U.S. Attorney's Offices in New York used the RICO statute for years against the Mafia, drug organizations, street gangs, and terrorist organizations. They continue to do so, as they are experts at RICO prosecutions. The New York prosecutors were very helpful to my AUSAs whenever they asked for advice and assistance. If your assigned AUSA has not prosecuted a RICO case, consider advising them to reach out to the New York U.S. Attorneys' Office for advice.

This reminds me of a very important point. Both RICO and VICAR target investigations require FBIHQ and U.S. DOJ approval prior to indictment. Although that may seem intimidating, the process was not difficult. It consisted of filling out the proper paperwork, and justifying the worthiness of your criminal enterprise or subject to be targeted by VICAR or RICO charges.

Just like anything else in life or investigations, the first one is the hardest. Look for cases in past prosecutions that were conducted by other investigators, or task forces to use as examples. To find the prior cases, turn to either FBIHQ or DOJ; they should be able to provide assistance.

The predicate acts under the RICO statute are numerous and can be seen in entirety in the Appendix; generally the most commonly used RICO predicate acts are drug offenses, bribery, sports bribery, counterfeiting, embezzlement of union funds, mail fraud, wire fraud, money laundering, obstruction of justice, murder for hire, drug trafficking, prostitution, sexual exploitation of children, alien smuggling, trafficking in counterfeit goods, theft from interstate shipment, interstate transportation of stolen property, and convictions of the following state crimes: murder, kidnapping, gambling, arson, robbery, bribery, extortion, and drugs.

Predicate acts on each subject can be as old as 20 years; however, one must be committed within the past 10 years. This requires a commitment of investigative resources to reviewing old cases tied to the criminal enterprise.

Be aware that the leaders that you are investigating today worked their way through the ranks of the criminal enterprise to become leaders. They had to "make their bones" and conduct criminal acts for the organization to prove themselves worthy. After they became bosses, they ordered criminal acts that were committed by the current lower- and middle-level members of the criminal enterprise.

This is the road map to RICO; once the enterprise has been identified and defined, the organizational charts documented and leaders identified, the investigation should concentrate a major part of their effort to identify and prove the criminal predicate acts.

Prior offenses are a treasure trove of intelligence and information regarding the leaders and the entire criminal enterprise. Spend time examining and evaluating prior offenses committed by the criminal enterprise. One of the advantages to investigating these predicate acts is if the subjects were already convicted of the crime in state court, they do not have to be retried in federal court. The AUSA just has to obtain a certified copy of the conviction and prove the subject did the act for the benefit of the criminal enterprise.

However, if other subjects are tied to the same predicate act and were not convicted in the original charge, they will have to be tried in federal court.

The elements of the crime for RICO are as follows:

1. Prove the criminal enterprise.
2. Prove the subject has committed "at least two acts of racketeering activity," drawn from a list of RICO crimes, within the past 20 years, with one in the past 10 years.

3. If the subject was convicted of the predicate act in state court, obtain certified copies of conviction. If not convicted in state court, prove the predicate offense beyond a reasonable doubt in federal court.
4. Prove the predicate acts were done for the benefit of the criminal enterprise.

In the NLR investigation, we conducted a review of crimes committed showed NLR members were involved in activities such as murder, attempted murder, assault with a deadly weapon, and numerous drug violations. Drug violations include the manufacture and distribution of methamphetamine, as well as violence and intimidation to collect "taxes" from other methamphetamine producers not working directly for the NLR.

Some of the predicate acts we used were offenses that we charged earlier in the NLR investigation. For example, three of the NLR subjects were indicted on federal charges of manufacture and distribution of methamphetamine, along with weapons charges.

Another NLR subject, "Hoss," was identified as a federal RICO target, and was to be charged and convicted with counts of attempted murder and robbery of a drug dealer who had been dealing methamphetamine to the NLR. Hoss attacked and beat the drug dealer with a Maglite and took his money and drugs. Later in the investigation, Snake, the NLR leader that approved Hoss's criminal activity, was included in the RICO charges.

The NLR investigation has also indicted and convicted two NLR members with VICAR, which had stemmed from the hate crime slashing (attempted murder) of a black inmate at the West Valley Detention Center. This incident indicated the NLR committed hate crimes because of their white supremacist philosophy. The NLR was closely associated with the Aryan Brotherhood (AB).

These affiliations and types of crimes assisted in defining the NLR as a criminal enterprise with a written code of conduct.

The hard work and persistence of the NLR Task Force eventually paid off. We eventually convicted 13 leaders of the NLR and had them shipped to federal prisons across the United States. We sent them away from their power base, which was the state prison system in California.

18 USC 1791: Providing or possessing contraband in prison

From Title 18—CRIMES AND CRIMINAL PROCEDURE
PART I—CRIMES
CHAPTER 87—PRISONS
§1791. Providing or possessing contraband in prison

(a) Offense—Whoever—
  (1) In violation of a statute or a rule or order issued under a statute, provides to an inmate of a prison a prohibited object, or attempts to do so; or
  (2) Being an inmate of a prison, makes, possesses, or obtains, or attempts to make or obtain, a prohibited object; shall be punished as provided in subsection (b) of this section (see Appendix for specific statutes).

If you are investigating a criminal enterprise, they will be conducting criminal activity and will eventually be incarcerated in federal or state prison. Leaders of the criminal enterprise may be powerful enough to maintain control of the criminal enterprise while incarcerated.

Although this statute applies directly to federal detention facilities, there are state laws that apply to contraband in state prisons. Crooks do not stop their crookery because they are in jail or prison. Their family members, associates, and other gang members will be caught with contraband, and this statute can be extremely valuable to you in the overall investigation.

The elements of the crime for possessing contraband in prison are as follows:

1. Possess or provides contraband to an inmate of a federal prison.
2. Prove the violation beyond a reasonable doubt in federal court.

Any leaders of the criminal enterprise that are incarcerated should be monitored closely. Since they are incarcerated and can be closely monitored, they will be subject to the rules of the facilities.

Make no mistake; there is a vast amount of intelligence that can be gathered during the leader's jail or prison stay.

For example, jails and prisons require visitors to register when they visit. These logs and the names they contain are valuable tools to assist in the identification of members and associates of the criminal enterprise.

The same applies to telephone records. The logs of the incarcerated criminal enterprise leader will lead to bolstering or further defining organizational charts.

The intelligence gleaned from telephone and visitor logs along with mail covers from jailed leaders can help break an investigation wide open.

For example, in the NLR investigation through monitoring incarcerated NLR members, we discovered the NLR was utilizing three-way calling networks through some of their associates. Telephone records from these associates were used to further identify targets and potential informants. Another useful investigative technique is to ask the institution to conduct a cell search of the incarcerated leader to look for contraband or intelligence in their personal possessions.

Be aware that this statute also includes charges for the person who provides the contraband, as well as the inmate who may eventually possess the contraband. These types of charges come in very handy when trying to persuade an associate or family member to become a potential informant or cooperating witness.

18 USC 521: Criminal street gangs

From Title 18—CRIMES AND CRIMINAL PROCEDURE
PART I—CRIMES
CHAPTER 26—CRIMINAL STREET GANGS
§521. Criminal street gangs

(a) Definitions
"Conviction" includes a finding, under state or federal law, that a person has committed an act of juvenile delinquency involving violent or controlled substances felony
"Criminal street gang" means an ongoing group, club, organization, or association of 5 or more persons—
(A) That has as 1 of its primary purposes the commission of 1 or more of the criminal offenses described in subsection (c);
(B) The members of which engage, or have engaged within the past 5 years, in a continuing series of offenses described in subsection (c); and
(C) The activities of which affect interstate or foreign commerce
"State" means a State of the United States, the District of Columbia, and any commonwealth, territory, or possession of the United States
(b) Penalty—The sentence of a person convicted of an offense described in subsection (c) shall be increased by up to 10 years if the offense is committed under the circumstances described in subsection (d)
(c) Offenses—The offenses described in this section are—
(1) a Federal felony involving a controlled substance (as defined in section 102 of the Controlled Substances Act (21 U.S.C. 802)) for which the maximum penalty is not less than 5 years;

(2) a Federal felony crime of violence that has as an element the use or attempted use of physical force against the person of another; and

(3) a Conspiracy to commit an offense described in paragraph (1) or (2)

(d) Circumstances—The circumstances described in this section are that the offense described in subsection (c) was committed by a person who—

(1) Participates in a criminal street gang with knowledge that its members engage in or have engaged in a continuing series of offenses described in subsection (c);

(2) Intends to promote or further the felonious activities of the criminal street gang or maintain or increase his or her position in the gang; and

(3) Has been convicted within the past 5 years for—

(A) An offense described in subsection (c);

(B) a State offense—

(i) Involving a controlled substance (as defined in section 102 of the Controlled Substances Act (21 U.S.C. 802)) for which the maximum penalty is not less than 5 years' imprisonment; or

(ii) that is a felony crime of violence that has as an element the use or attempted use of physical force against the person of another;

(C) Any Federal or State felony offense that by its nature involves a substantial risk that physical force against the person of another may be used in the course of committing the offense; or

(D) a Conspiracy to commit an offense described in subparagraph (A), (B), or (C)

This statute was written specifically to target street gangs. Although this statute is not one that I have personally utilized in any of my investigations, I wish that I had the chance to use it. It was not in effect when I was working street gangs.

Upon close scrutiny, this statute is a mini-RICO statute specific to street gangs. The penalties include the addition of 10 years in prison to any offense that the subject is convicted of in either federal or state court. This statute enhances the sentences of subjects upon conviction and is somewhat similar to the use of a firearm in commission of a crime under Title 18 Section 924 (c).

The elements of the crime for criminal street gangs are as follows:

1. Prove the "criminal street gang" exists as a functioning organization of five or more persons.
2. Prove the gang affected interstate or foreign commerce.
3. Prove the federal or state crime was a violent felony and/or a drug trafficking crime.
4. Prove the subject is a member of the criminal street gang.
5. Prove the subject committed the crime for the benefit of the gang.
6. Prove the subject committed the offense beyond a reasonable doubt in federal court.

Knowing the statutes and the elements of the crime that must be proven in court allows the investigator to gather the evidence during crucial stages of the investigation.

For example, if one of the elements of the crime is to prove the criminal act was perpetrated for the benefit of the criminal enterprise, the investigator should include questions in any interviews with key subjects that address the element of the crime at the time of the subjects arrest and interview, the initial arrest interview being the most important. It is usually the only chance to interview the subject in the modern criminal justice system. Knowing the right questions to ask at the right time can make or break a case.

Educate yourself and the task force on the statutes that you may be utilizing to disrupt and dismantle the targeted criminal enterprise. The more versed you are in the federal statutes and what you have to prove through effective investigation, the less likely that you and your task force will have to run helter-skelter at the midnight hour prior to a VICAR or RICO indictment.

Know the elements of the crime and prove them as you are investigating "real time," it will only make your life easier.

14

Vulnerabilities

This chapter concentrates on identifying the vulnerabilities of the targeted criminal enterprise.

Where is the organization weak? Where are the openings for investigators to infiltrate the organization? Where can we develop witnesses or informants? Is there a criminal activity that has been punished at one level be exploited? For example, as stated earlier, early in the NLR investigation, a felon with a gun on parole was a six-month violation at the state level. But research and application soon discovered an applicable federal statute to a felon in possession of a firearm. The federal charge carried a 10-year penalty without a chance for parole. This was a substantial difference that we were able to use to our advantage in the NLR investigation.

Are there elements of the organization that can be infiltrated? Where are the opportunities to utilize sophisticated investigative techniques?

For example, investigation showed that NLR members were utilizing three-way calls from prison to conduct NLR criminal activity in and out of prison. We found an NLR associate operated a three-way calling base for NLR members and compiled a $21,000 phone bill in a five-month period. We discovered vulnerabilities that we exploited. Here is how the three-way calling investigation played out.

The FBI and SSU conducted a parole search on the three-way caller's residence. The three-way caller had been indemnified through contact with incarcerated NLR members. Her sister was on state parole. Both of them had NLR contacts. We searched the house to obtain intelligence and evidence. Two NLR members have been arrested at that residence based on cooperating witness information. Other telephone targets were identified. Their telephone numbers were being targeted for pen registers with a goal of obtaining court-ordered electronic surveillance.

To exploit this identified vulnerability, FBI case agents utilized pre-paid cellular telephones, which were handed off to worthy NLR targets to conduct drug and NLR business. Case agents handed off the phone through credible cooperating witness sources to NLR members, in an attempt to obtain a pen register and develop probable cause for a Title III wiretap.

The NLR was exposed and vulnerable by utilizing the three-way calling system. We developed a vast amount of intelligence from the three was calling network; it was worthy of the resources we devoted to exploit the vulnerability.

One of the most fruitful vulnerabilities that we pursued in the NLR investigation was targeting old girl friends of NLR members and developing them as informants and cooperating witnesses.

Every one of the NLR members we investigated was on state parole. The SSU had access to past and real-time intelligence on the NLR from all the state prisons across California. The NLR communication methods included word of mouth and written notes smuggled out of prison by trusted NLR members and associates. Once we identified a communication method, it was immediately evaluated for exploitation.

When investigating your criminal enterprise ask yourself this question. How can you get into their communications stream unnoticed and monitor their most secret communications?

Identifying vulnerabilities in a targeted criminal enterprises finances and communication systems can be critical pathways to a successful investigation. Criminal enterprises require effective communications and a robust financial system to operate on a daily basis. The leaders must have the ability to issue orders to the rank and file. Then they must have a credible method of payment for deeds carried out regarding their orders. Without an effective communication and financial network, a criminal enterprise will quickly lose its credibility. A criminal enterprise that can't communicate or pay the bills is doomed.

What is the point of this chapter? It is to find the vulnerabilities of the targeted criminal enterprise, especially in the areas of communications and finance, and exploit these vulnerabilities to disrupt and dismantle the organization.

Keep one thing in mind, as you identify the inner workings of the criminal enterprise communications and financial networks, they will evolve.

In other words, like the three-way calling example with the NLR, once they knew we had raided the three-way callers' house, they stopped three-way calling and moved on to using other methods of communications.

The search for vulnerabilities is a constant mission that must evolve with the criminals and their criminal activity.

15

Informants and
Information Sources

One cannot underestimate the worth of insiders who are turned against the targeted criminal enterprise. One of the most important questions that should be asked early and daily throughout the investigation is, "Who and where are the most valuable potential informants?"

Finding valuable insiders within the criminal enterprise will almost always break the investigation wide open. They are the ones who know the "who, what, where, and when" of the enterprise.

While identifying the leadership, members, and people associated with the criminal enterprise, investigators and analysts must be on a constant watch for the right circumstances in the investigation to approach and exploit vulnerabilities of these individuals. Find the criminal's weaknesses, target them, and exploit their weaknesses to turn the criminal subject into the cooperating witness.

To make it perfectly clear, when I say to find their weaknesses and target them, I am talking about thoroughly investigating the potential informants. Find charges that can be levied against them. Charge them as subjects, and then try to convince them to cooperate for a reduced sentence or dismissal of charges.

Understand there are two types of people that you will be targeting in your investigation: principal subjects and potential informants. "Remember all of them start out as subjects." Expect that as you develop RICO, VICAR, and CCE charges on the leaders of the criminal enterprise that some of the leaders will cooperate for a reduction in charges or sentences. The leaders of these criminal enterprises are generally survivors. Once the indictments are imminent, they will rush to get the best deal.

Informants can be found at any level of the targeted criminal enterprise. Opportunities may include girlfriends, family members, associates, and all levels of criminal enterprise membership.

As an example, an opportunity may present itself if the daughter of the criminal enterprise accountant is arrested for a felony that may result in a lengthy term of incarceration.

Investigators and analysts must evaluate the value of the accountant to the investigation and future prosecution. If the accountant's knowledge and evidence is deemed to be invaluable investigators should consider an approach to the district attorney. Propose a deal for the daughter that can be presented to the accountant to persuade the accountant to cooperate in the criminal enterprise investigation. Approach the accountant with the deal and try to persuade him to cooperate.

The well-placed insider is the "golden goose" to any criminal investigation, especially one who knows the enterprise inside out and decides to fully cooperate. Building ironclad cases on the potential informants is essential to ensure their cooperation. Remember the potential informant or cooperating witness has been a criminal all their life, and cooperating with you is the last thing they ever thought they would be doing. They will always want to get back to the life that many of them grew into, and some will be cooperating on their own family members. They cannot be trusted unless they are cooperating to save their own hides. The deals struck with the informants and cooperating witnesses must be documented and strict standards must be set for them to meet to complete the deal. Then they must be monitored to ensure they are indeed meeting the standards. Trust but verify.

Do not overlook the enemies of the criminal enterprise, as they can be valuable sources against your targets. If your criminal enterprise is at war with another criminal enterprise and any subjects of the rival organization is arrested, they may be all too happy to provide information on their enemies.

Make sure that you coordinate with the agency that arrested the person you are interviewing and/or any task force that may be working the rival criminal enterprise. You do not want other investigators talking to or making deals with your subjects, so be professional and conduct the proper due diligence.

One of the drug informants that I had was good at installing hidden compartments in cars for drug traffickers. The hidden compartments were works of art and almost impossible to detect in a vehicle as the hidden compartments were electronically activated. The informant would install the hidden compartments in vehicles for a set fee and the customers would range across several drug trafficking organizations.

The informant would contact the task force and let us know he had an order for a hidden compartment and give us a name of a subject. We would identify the subject through investigation.

Once the informant finished the hidden compartment, he would show us how it worked and give us the vehicle for a day. We would install a hidden tracking device in the vehicle and track the subject's movement through the vehicle.

Our drug investigations were successful. We would use the tracker in the vehicle as a starting point for surveillance. We would identify stash houses and hand off the stash houses to a completely different law enforcement team. They would begin an independent surveillance and develop independent probable cause for a search warrant. The system was quite successful and many people were arrested because of our efforts. The informant eventually was arrested himself and was no longer useful to us.

Much later, we found out that the informant was only giving us a small percentage of the vehicles that he was altering. If he was slighted or crossed in any way the vehicle would come to the task force. He was using the police to get revenge on anyone that pissed him off.

This brings me to the point of discussion as to what motivates a subject to become an informant.

There are generally two types of informants: (1) those who are working with the police to reduce charges/sentences and (2) those who are motivated by money. A word of caution on informants is that they are purely motivated by money. There are professional informants out there that will work for several agencies at the same time.

For example, an informant meets with a young FBI agent in the morning. The agent asks the informant several questions regarding his drug investigations. The agent's questions include specific facts about his investigations, such as Have you heard anything about Jose dealing cocaine out of the La Hacienda restaurant on 54th Street? How about T-Bone from the Piru Bloods, is he still living in the Motel 6 off Crenshaw and 83rd Street? No, the informant answers. He doesn't know anything about Jose or T-Bone.

Nevertheless, in the afternoon the informant meets with the DEA agent he has been working with for years. The first words out of the informant's mouth are these: I have information on Jose who is dealing coke out of the La Hacienda restaurant on 54th Street. Oh, and by the way, T-Bone is still dealing crack out of the Motel 6 off Crenshaw and 83rd Street. The DEA pays the informant.

If the DEA asks the informant any specific questions the next time he meets with the FBI, he reports it as firsthand information. The FBI pays the informant, a very dirty and stained cycle of circular reporting. The informant who is motivated strictly on a monetary basis must be worked with an abundance of caution.

Criminals that are working off charges can be held to a measurable standard. The deal can be revoked if they do not meet the criteria set for them in any written agreement drafted by the AUSA.

This is called "holding a hammer" over the subjects head. Subjects who are charged throughout the investigation should be evaluated for potential as a cooperating witness or an informant.

If the subjects you are investigating are career criminals with lengthy criminal records, they will be difficult to turn against their own without substantial charges levied against them. However, the smart ones will "roll" as soon as RICO indictments are handed down. Everyone knows that the first to the table gets the best deal.

Developing and working informants is science and art combined. There are certain traits and indicators that can be identified that may be exploited to roll an informant. However, potential informants are people, and there is no telling what one person will do when put in a compromising situation.

So, my advice is to try to roll everyone that may be of value to your investigation. Make sure you don't give the best deals to the leaders of your criminal enterprise and pound the lower level members. The leaders will be out of prison in a short time and reestablish the criminal enterprise.

Follow the rules and do it right. Treat the subjects with respect and dignity. Do not lie or promise things that you can't deliver.

Always be friendly with the informants and cooperating witnesses but "always" remember that they are not your friends! No informant can ever be trusted.

If there is one rule that you remember from this book, remember this rule, you should always be friendly with your informants to build rapport, "but never forget they are not your real friends." Don't socialize with informants off duty. Never bring them to your house. Never talk about your family to them. They make their living exploiting weaknesses, just as we do in our investigations. Do not expose your personal vulnerabilities to them. They will compromise you. Remain courteous but always remain professional. Make sure you let them know who is in charge. You are in charge, not them. Avoid the road to disaster by controlling your informants!

Be aware these people have turned on their families and fellow criminals, so do not trust them. They will turn on you if it appears to benefit them. Do not allow them to set meeting places. Certainly do not allow them to compromise you or fellow officer safety for the sake of not wanting to offend them.

If discovered or even suspected as being a "rat" by a violent criminal enterprise, the first step by the informant may be to set up an ambush on you or your task force.

16

Finances

Regardless of the form, ideology, structure, motivations, or ethnic background of the criminal enterprise, there is one common denominator to the most diverse criminal organizations: money. Finances drive the legitimate business world and play a chief role in the criminal world.

When examining criminal enterprises, it is easy to concentrate on the violent acts that are conducted by the members or associates of the organization. However, on closer examination, you will see the violent acts are usually rare compared to money making-related crimes. The business of the criminal enterprise is to make money every day, at every opportunity possible.

Oftentimes, the violent acts are committed because someone dealing with the criminal enterprise did not meet their financial commitment to the organization. An example is often made of that person; they are killed or beat down to show others that the criminal enterprise is not to be trifled with to ensure the bills owed were paid on time.

The following statute relates to money laundering and can be used effectively against a criminal enterprise that is hiding money gained from illegal activity.

There are several other federal statutes pertaining to finances, including wire fraud, mail fraud, and forfeiture laws, that can be very useful in the disruption of the daily operations of the criminal enterprise.

18 USC 1956: Laundering of monetary instruments

From Title 18—CRIMES AND CRIMINAL PROCEDURE
PART I—CRIMES
CHAPTER 95—RACKETEERING
§1956. Laundering of monetary instruments

(a) (1) Whoever, knowing that the property involved in a financial transaction represents the proceeds of some form of unlawful activity, conducts or attempts to conduct such a financial transaction which in fact involves the proceeds of specified unlawful activity—

(A) (i) With the intent to promote the carrying on of specified unlawful activity; or

(ii) with intent to engage in conduct constituting a violation of Section 7201 or 7206 of the Internal Revenue Code of 1986; or

(B) Knowing that the transaction is designed in whole or in part-

(i) To conceal or disguise the nature, the location, the source, the ownership, or the control of the proceeds of specified unlawful activity; or

(ii) to avoid a transaction reporting requirement under State or Federal law, shall be sentenced to a fine of not more than $500,000 or twice the value of the property involved in the transaction, whichever is greater, or imprisonment for not more than twenty years, or both. For purposes of this paragraph, a financial transaction shall be considered to be one involving the proceeds of specified unlawful activity if it is part of a set of parallel or dependent transactions, any one of which involves the proceeds of specified unlawful activity, and all of which are part of a single plan or arrangement

(2) Whoever transports, transmits, or transfers, or attempts to transport, transmit, or transfer a monetary instrument or funds from a place in the United States to or through a place outside the United States or to a place in the United States from or through a place outside the United States—

(A) With the intent to promote the carrying on of specified unlawful activity; or

(B) Knowing that the monetary instrument or funds involved in the transportation, transmission, or transfer represent the proceeds of some form of unlawful activity and knowing that such transportation, transmission, or transfer is designed in whole or in part—

(i) To conceal or disguise the nature, the location, the source, the ownership, or the control of the proceeds of specified unlawful activity; or

(ii) to avoid a transaction reporting requirement under State or Federal law, shall be sentenced to a fine of not more than $500,000 or twice the value of the monetary instrument or funds involved in the transportation, transmission, or transfer, whichever is greater, or imprisonment for not more than twenty years, or both. For the purpose of the offense described in subparagraph (B), the defendant's knowledge may be established by proof that a law enforcement officer represented the matter specified in subparagraph (B) as true, and the defendant's subsequent statements or actions indicate that the defendant believed such representations to be true.

As you can see from reading the money laundering statute, it was written to prevent criminals from hiding money they make from their illegal activity.

There are two major parts to the statute. The first one deals with trying to hide funds obtained through illegal activity by manipulating bank accounts and transactions. The second part of the statute deals with funneling the illegally obtained cash out of or through the United States.

There are certain state and federal reporting requirements regarding monetary transactions. If the criminals avoid these requirements and you can prove it, they are subject to fines and seizure of their funds.

The two parts of the elements of the crime of money laundering are as follows:

1. Prove the subject was obtaining funds illegally.
2. Prove intent.
3. Prove the crime involved a financial transaction meant to promote the illegal activity and one or more of the following:
   A. To avoid paying taxes to the IRS
   B. To hide ownership of the funds
   C. To avoid other state or federal reporting requirements
4. Prove the subject committed the offense beyond a reasonable doubt in federal court.

The second part of the money laundering statute is as follows:

1. Prove the subject moved money internationally to continue the criminal activity.
2. Prove intent.
3. Prove the crime involved a financial transaction meant to promote the illegal activity and one or more of the following:
   A.   To hide ownership of the funds
   B.   To avoid other state or federal reporting requirements
4. Prove the subject committed the offense beyond a reasonable doubt in federal court.

So when you are investigating the targeted criminal enterprise start asking yourself several questions. How is the enterprise making money and/or valuables? How is the enterprise distributing money and/or valuables? How is the enterprise tracking money and/or valuables?

In many criminal enterprises, cash is king. Unlike bank transactions, cash is hard to trace and it gets instant results. Of course, a large amount of cash also opens the criminal enterprise to certain risks and vulnerabilities.

Dealing in cash can be dangerous, as there are always people outside the organization who are willing to take a chance on a large score of money by robbing the criminal enterprise of large sums of cash, either through direct action or through sham drug deals.

These types of actions were commonplace in the 1990s, and even powerful MDTOs had to add extra security measures against robbers and kidnappers.

The other side of the coin in dealing with cash is the temptation to insiders: organization members and associates of the criminal enterprise. Dealing in millions of dollars in cash on a daily basis leads to even the most loyal people looking to supplement their income through skimming off some of the profits.

Dealing with insiders who steal their money will always be a problem for criminal enterprises that deal in cash. Of course, to the savvy investigator, there is a potential avenue to develop informants who rip off the criminal enterprise and are discovered.

You will need to get them before the criminal enterprise does and kills them. In addition, since they will be on the outs with the criminal enterprise, their information will be historical.

In dealing with cash, the tracking from the street level to the coffers of the MDTO could be difficult. A tracking system must be in place to ensure the dollar made on the street ends up in the hands of the leaders of the criminal enterprise. Whatever the tracking system be that is generic to your criminal enterprise, it is imperative that resources be devoted to identifying the methods and persons responsible for tracking the funds of the criminal enterprise. They will know the methods of taking in the money and distributing it to the members and associates of the criminal enterprise. Getting these individuals to cooperate with the task force should be a primary focus of the investigation.

Loyalty to the organization demands people get paid for their efforts. The credibility of any enterprise, criminal or legitimate, depends on the ability to pay people working for them and paying on time, on a regular basis.

One of the best ways to disrupt the activities of the targeted criminal enterprise is to find their methods of financing their operations and focusing resources to concentrate on investigating these finances.

Section III

Investigation

17

Overt

There are two investigative paths that you can take when you decide to dismantle a targeted criminal enterprise: covert or overt. Covert entails investigators of the criminal enterprise working behind the scenes. They take every effort to ensure secrecy of the efforts to dismantle the criminal enterprise through RICO charges. Since the crooks commit crimes and are convicted at the state level, there will be past cases to examine for potential RICO predicate acts on the leaders of the criminal enterprise. The process calls for secretive and unseen investigative efforts. The covert investigators take every pain, so that the criminals do not know they are being investigated.

On the other hand, the overt investigation is generally known to the members of the criminal enterprise. They know you are coming for them. In addition to RICO charges meant to dismantle the criminal enterprise, the overt investigators use low-level street and/or financial crimes to disrupt the criminal enterprise's daily operations. They watch for crimes to charge potential sources and convince them to cooperate. They stay on the members and associates of the criminal enterprise, keeping up the pressure once applied, while at the same time conducting a RICO investigation on the leaders of the organization.

The NLR Task Force was overt. During the course of the investigation, NLR Task Force team members utilized every investigative tool available to effectively disrupt and dismantle the NLR.

The investigative strategy included using parole searches and search warrants to develop charges against lower level NLR members meant to "roll" them to testify against the leadership of the NLR.

But if an NLR member agreed to testify, he was brought to the FGJ as soon as possible to "lock in" his testimony. This tactic kept NLR Task Force investigators "on the street." These tactics also provided suppression of the NLR daily operations.

Besides the state charges, the NLR Task Force also charged any NLR members with federal charges, especially weapons charges. The NLR liked guns. The gun charges carried hefty penalties and were brought to bear against NLR leaders in an attempt to keep NLR leadership off balance and disrupt NLR effectiveness. This approach was aimed at depleting the NLR leadership power base.

Over the period of two years, the NLR Task Force compiled the following statistical accomplishments: 11 federal arrests, 3 federal complaints, 27 federal indictments (including 12 RICO indictments), 35 federal convictions, and 254 state arrests.

The objective of the investigation was to dismantle the NLR gang as a criminal enterprise through federal RICO and VICAR convictions. The overall objective was to indict the top NLR leadership on RICO charges to totally disrupt the NLR as an organization. As you can see from the statistics of the NLR Task Force, there were a dozen RICO charges on the leadership that took three years to investigate. But look at the state arrests, over 250 arrests in two years. This was the disruption phase of the investigation. The RICO indictments were returned on the NLR leadership on December 13, 2002.

After we found crimes that the NLR was conducting as part of their daily operations, we targeted those crimes for investigation. I already mentioned the gun charges. Another favorite criminal scheme that the NLR leaders preferred was the concept of "taxing" drug dealers that were not affiliated with the NLR but were manufacturing and distributing methamphetamine in the NLR territory. The drug dealers were forced to pay tribute to the NLR each month for drugs sold by these independent drug dealers. Refusal to pay resulted in beat downs or robbery by NLR members.

As stated earlier, the NLR member "Hoss" attacked and beat a drug dealer with a Maglite, causing serve head injury and putting him in the hospital. Hoss also robbed him, taking his money and drugs. Hoss was convicted of the VICAR for this assault. Later when we were building a RICO case on the NLR, we utilized this VICAR conviction as a RICO predicate act on another NLR leader "Snake." On one occasion, we had gathered evidence that Snake had ordered a general order to hit any drug dealers for not paying taxes to the NLR for dealing methamphetamine in their territory. Snake was charged with this attempted murder and several other offenses, including murder in the overall RICO case.

Of the 250 state arrests, the majority of them were for drug offenses and violent crimes relating to NLR operations. These street-level operations were the main stay of the disruption phase of the investigation. Targeting the base of the NLR's organization allowed the NLR Task Force to understand the NLR. To learn firsthand how the NLR was operating and who they were working with to conduct their criminal activity.

The experience and education of the task force members throughout the disruption phase of the investigation could not have been obtained any other way. By the end of the three-year investigation, every NLR Task Force member was an expert on the NLR. We all knew who the NLR leaders were, how they got to their positions, their enemies, friends, and associates. We knew the NLR vulnerabilities and financial structure, and we knew how to exploit their weaknesses and developed an excellent informant base.

I personally prefer the overt investigative technique. But I do understand the covert approach.

The hands-on approach allows the task force to develop the expertise they need to become true experts through interaction with the people and organizations they are investigating.

An additional advantage to working the street crimes together as a task force is the small unit cohesion that develops from working together in sometimes harsh conditions. There is a strong bond that develops between people who have been in dangerous situations and came through together.

Personal preference or circumstances may lead a task force to choose the overt investigative technique. The rewards of the closely knit effective and efficient task force are indescribable.

18

Covert

There are instances where the investigation may need to be covert. I have also worked cases where it was necessary to keep the subjects of the criminal enterprise from knowing they were being investigated until the final indictment. The subjects were members of a criminal enterprise that was large and sophisticated enough to relocate from one area to another if they found out they were being investigated. They were well funded and could relocate key members within a very short period. Many of the MDTO investigations in the 1990s and the Los Angeles ATF investigation on the Aryan Brotherhood were conducted as covert investigations.

Just because the investigation is covert, it doesn't mean there isn't an ongoing investigation; it is not all historical. Oftentimes, the criminal enterprise is apprehensive at the mention of the "feds." Whether be it the FBI, DEA, or ATF, the criminals do not usually come in contact with federal investigators on a daily basis. However, they expect members of their criminal enterprise to come in contact with the local and state police.

Therefore, covert means the crooks don't know the feds have a RICO investigation targeting their criminal enterprise. In a covert case, there may be no ongoing federal grand jury investigation.

The investigators will generally filter information to the local or state police or take out portions of the enterprise without mentioning federal agency involvement. These techniques are useful in certain circumstances but call for extreme attentiveness to information flow. This technique makes it somewhat difficult when trying to form a task force. The leaders of the departments who you wish to recruit as task force participants will want briefings and detailed information on what their officers will be doing as task force members.

Conversely, the more people who know about the investigation, the less likely that it will stay covert for very long.

On the other hand, it is extremely difficult to build trust with fellow law enforcement agencies whenever the words "I can't share that with you" are spoken. That is why many of the covert investigations consist of one or two agents from the same agency operating secretly in the shadows. The more people who know about the investigation, the more likely the secret will get back to the targeted criminals.

The two techniques are very similar in one aspect. The covert investigation is mostly historical and is dependent on past crimes to compile a RICO case against the leadership of the organization. The overt investigation also utilizes the past criminal activity to compile a RICO case against the targeted criminal enterprise leadership.

The difference comes with the disruption phase of the overt investigative technique. By targeting the street-level offenses of the criminal enterprise, the task force is certain to make its presence and intentions known. The covert operation rarely is directly involved in street-level operations and operates in the shadow realm of historical cases.

Make no mistake; the impact of the covert operation is as significant as the overt operation. The dismantlement of the targeted criminal enterprise through the utilization of RICO charges is the ultimate goal of both investigative techniques.

One final point regarding the overt and covert investigative techniques is that there have been some federal cases where the investigation has been covert due to the use of a deep undercover agent who was operating in the criminal enterprise.

The ATF ran several successful undercover operations against several motorcycle gangs. The FBI used deep undercover agents against the Mafia in the past. Nevertheless, use of the undercover operation does not mean the investigation of the criminal enterprise has to be strictly covert. The undercover technique can be used parallel with overt techniques.

The occasional raid or arrest of a member of the organization is a guarantee that the rest of the members will be discussing the arrest and developing new ways to ensure they don't get arrested for the same offense. It is similar to tickling the wire in a wiretap investigation.

The bottom line is the dismantlement of the criminal enterprise. The mission can be accomplished whether the techniques are covert or overt.

19

Sophisticated Investigative Techniques

The use of sophisticated investigative techniques can be a productive and creative way to disrupt and dismantle the targeted criminal enterprise. These techniques usually refer to communication intercepts and undercover operations (UCO).

I have utilized both techniques. There is great value to both techniques. I personally prefer the undercover cases. However, my personal experience with wire taps came before the explosion of social media.

Texting on smartphones, Facebook, Twitter, LinkedIn, and other methods of communication have opened a cornucopia of information to the investigator.

If I was still working cases, I would definitely explore the laws and see how to exploit the information that is available through social media.

Over the three-year period of the NLR investigation, we did utilize a wiretap and explored several undercover avenues. The sophisticated investigative techniques didn't provide a huge breakthrough in the overall investigation, which depended on regular investigation. However, I know of several successful FBI cases that depended solely on wiretaps.

I have successfully employed undercover techniques in several other FBI investigations.

Please be clear when I say the sophisticated investigative techniques we used in the NLR case did not produce home runs; they did assist in the investigative effort. The sophisticated techniques in the NLR investigation did provide evidence that was used to prove the criminal enterprise in the

RICO and VICAR trials. Cameras captured and recorded the organized physical training the NLR conducted on a regular basis. This training was led by the senior NLR member and was conducted in formation similar to the military. The video turned out to be a powerful piece of evidence of their criminal enterprise.

Many of the NLR leaders and their associates were incarcerated in Palm Hall, Chino Institute for Men. They were segregated and locked down a majority of the time. They were allowed to congregate on the Palm Hall recreation yard on Sunday, Monday, and Thursday from 9:00 a.m. to 11:00 a.m. FBI technical trained agents (TTA) installed a digital video camera at the Palm Hall recreation yard with monitoring equipment terminating at the Riverside Resident Agency.

The TTAs developed a method to install audio equipment in the Palm Hall recreation hall to record NLR subject's conversation as they are on recreation time. AUSA Olmedo had been consulted in this matter. Eventually, a federal wiretap affidavit was written by the investigators and obtained from Department of Justice by AUSA Olmedo.

The NLR subjects conducted business on the yard and recording their conversations was valuable. Some evidence was gathered that was used in the RICO trials, but it was not the treasure trove of information that we expected.

An undercover idea explored in the NLR case was through a cooperating witness (CW) who had been developed that was in a position to meet with NLR members "on the street" in San Bernardino County. The CW was a NLR member in good standing with numerous NLR contacts, including many of the RICO targets of this investigation. An UCO was considered and the groundwork for a Group II UCO was developed. Unfortunately, the CW was arrested and the UCO was not implemented.

The plan was to initiate the UCO out of a small industrial complex. The "shop" was to be equipped with CCTV and audio recording equipment and provided a meeting place for NLR members to discuss NLR business, which was to be recorded by task force members. The CW was to act as a "fence" for stolen merchandise from NLR members and associates. AUSA Olmedo was consulted and concurred with the use of the undercover technique.

Another separate UCO was considered in this NLR investigation. Plans for a Group I or Group II UCO that would have operated out of a small industrial office complex or an undercover apartment were evaluated.

Local police department contacts were in a position to provide, free of charge, undercover apartments for a period of three months that could be wired by the FBI to determine if the UCO will provide a meeting place for the NLR to hold meetings that will be covered by CCTV.

An undercover agent or officer was to be introduced that could have provided a three-way calling base for the NLR and provided NLR leaders with cellular telephones, pagers, and other equipment that can be monitored by the FBI.

The UCO was also to be used as a "fence" where NLR members and associates can sell stolen property to the undercover agent. Again this UCO was not implemented because of logistical and resource restrictions.

The NLR examples were of the exploration of sophisticated investigative techniques that were not as successful as it was hoped they would be in the overall investigation.

However, the application of these techniques educated the entire NLR Task Force staff. The techniques also paved the way for their use by these investigators in similar cases in the future. The effort was not in vain.

The experience of obtaining the NLR Title III wiretap affidavit was especially valuable to one of the young FBI agents. He was later transferred to Porto Rico. He used his experience to stand up several successful wiretaps on a notorious gang in Porto Rico. His investigation led to the arrest and conviction of several leaders of the gang.

20

Put It All Together
Investigate

This chapter concentrates on investigative tools and models to target a criminal enterprise operating in your area of responsibility. It is a synopsis of the major points we have covered until now. It's time to put these things together and disrupt/dismantle the targeted criminal enterprise. So let's recap and review the investigative stages of our endeavor (Figure 20.1).

Identify problem—What enterprise are we going to target and why? What are the objectives? What is the end game? Criminal activity? Political motivations? Potential for violence?

Build law enforcement working group—Who are we going to ask for assistance? Who has interest in seeing this enterprise dismantled? Where are the subjects operating? Federal, state, and local entities may have some interest in part or all of the investigation. How about parole and probation? A working group doesn't have any formalization like a task force.

Politics—Be aware that each agency has mission needs and motivation for either assisting you in your efforts or not. Make sure you treat other agencies with respect and attempt to fulfill their needs through membership on the task force.

Prosecutors—Do your best to find and latch onto the best federal, state, and local prosecutors for your investigation. Remember you can't keep criminals in jail if they aren't convicted through the efforts of aggressive and passionate prosecutors.

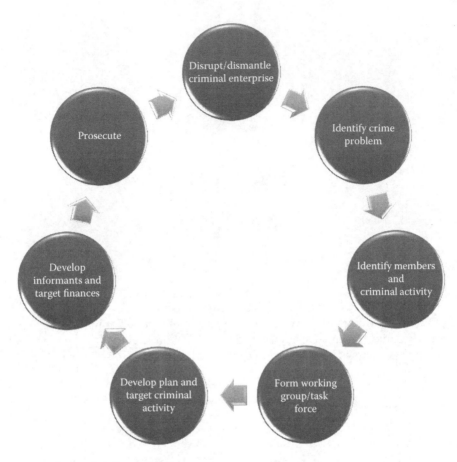

Figure 20.1 CEI flowchart.

Basic training—Working group members must be evaluated and trained in basic investigative techniques. Interviewing, report writing, and basic investigative skills must be set to a high standard, and officers must meet those standards. Team training can assist in real team building.

Engage community—Communities such as church groups, youth groups, housing authority, and civic groups must be engaged during investigation.

Define enterprise—What is an enterprise? There is a difference between two subjects entering into a conspiracy to commit a specific crime and two guys who commit crimes to contribute resources to their mutual partnership. Describe what constitutes an organization and an enterprise.

Develop organizational chart—Who are the leaders? Who are the mid-level managers? Who are the low-level players? Associates? Family members?

Research criminal activity—What are they doing that is illegal? What is their jurisdiction? International, federal, state, or local? Review and become familiar with statutes and the elements of the crimes that they are committing. Know what is to be proven and how to prove it.

Informants and sources—Explain the value of insiders, that is, those who know the "who, what, where, and when" of the enterprise. Find their weaknesses and target them, such as girlfriends, family members, associates, and all levels of enterprise memberships. Do not overlook enemies; they could be valuable sources against your targeted criminal enterprise.

Finances—How is the enterprise making, distributing, and tracking money and/or valuables? Loyalty to the organization demands people get paid for their efforts.

Vulnerabilities—Where is the organization weak? What criminal activity has been punished at one level that can be escalated? For example, in the past, a felon with a gun on parole was a six-month violation at the state level, but your task force has discovered that the same crime is a ten-year felony at the federal level—very impactful.

Formalize task force—When the working group has been together for a while, formalize into a task force. Formal federal task force has benefits. One of the benefits includes overtime for local officers. Formal task force oversight is the closest guarantee that the best officers are dedicated to the task force.

Target leaders and their successors—Identify the leaders and the middle-level subjects that get things done. Go after them with a passion and driven persistence.

Disruption:

    Overt—Use low-level street and/or financial crimes to disrupt the enterprise daily operations. Watch for crimes to charge potential sources. Stay on them and keep up the pressure once applied.

    Covert—Filter information to the local or state police to take out portions of the enterprise.

> *Dismantlement*—Utilize RICO and VICAR charges on leaders and
> middle-level managers of the enterprise to dismantle their
> activities and operations.

Throughout this book, I have used the NLR case that we completed as an
example. From the point that the NLR was identified as a crime problem,
I applied the techniques described in this book to investigate the NLR.

In the beginning, we had some issues to work through between our
member agencies. The politics of jurisdictional law enforcement worked
through we formalized the NLR Task Force, the members ended up being
the FBI, SSU, OPD, UPD and FPD, and the ATF.

We had a top-notch AUSA, and AUSA Olmedo made our lives easy as
investigators. She was hardworking, passionate about the case, and a true
team player. Defining the enterprise consisted of obtaining written by law
of the NLR and witness testimony in the FGJ that described who the NLR
was and what they stood for as an organization.

Once we defined the enterprise, identified the NLR leaders, and were
familiar with their criminal activity, we set goals and objectives to disrupt
and dismantle the NLR.

We focused on a two-pronged approach to disrupt their daily operations through enforcement targeting street-level crimes. We also utilized
RICO and VICAR statutes against their leaders to dismantle their
organization.

Our focus was maintained through a written mission statement that
the entire task force understood. Members of the task force executive
management were briefed every three months. The police departments
appreciated the candor and being kept in the loop. After the initial misun-
derstanding, effective communication was key to our success.

When the investigative portion of the NLR transitioned to the prosecutive stages, all task force members assisted in ensuring successful
prosecutions.

Witnesses in the NLR court cases consisted of law enforcement experts
on the NLR and NLR members that we had turned into cooperating witnesses. We operated dozens of informants and cooperating witnesses
developed during the three-year investigative period. Some of them were
caught committing criminal acts and were dealt with appropriately.

The key is building a good team that can work together for a common
cause. A good team can overcome almost any obstacles. On the opposite
side of the coin, one bad apple can create roadblock and hamper daily
operations.

Don't allow any team members to sway from the overall mission. Make sure your members understand that dalliance is an anomaly, not the way the task force is going to conduct business. They must adhere to the mission.

Once you are confident in your task force members understanding of the mission, launch into the investigation with a passion. If you are the federal agent in charge of the task force, lead by example.

If the task force is out late on an important case, ensure you make every effort to be there with them. Initially, it will be important for you to go out every time that they do, to demonstrate your passion and ability.

Once you have won their respect you can prioritize the cases that you go out on. Do not burn yourself out. There will be cases that they can handle without you. You just have to get to know them, how they think, and what is important to each of them.

Remember this saying that I learned in the U.S. Army, "Mission first, men always"; always take care of your troops. However, ensure that they understand, as long as they are on the task force, that the task force mission must be paramount.

Once you know who the people you are targeting and the type of criminal activity they are conducting, the investigation will take on its own personality.

Although similar, I haven't seen two investigations that were exactly the same. Stay flexible enough and adjust to investigation specifics on a case-by-case basis. The simple formula is once you know whom you are going after; identify what they are doing, and go after them with everything that is available to you and the task force. Make sure you get them through legal and ethical investigation.

Build cases at every level: federal, state, and local. The classic example is Al Capone. He was the largest gangster in the country during Prohibition. Everyone knew that Capone was bootlegging liquor and ordering violent acts such as extortion, arson, shootings, assaults, and murder, but after years of investigation, it was the charges of income tax evasion that sent him to prison and broke up his criminal enterprise.

The point to this story is to build as many cases as you can against the leaders of the criminal enterprise. You don't know which charges will be provable to court standards, so put a lot of arrows in your quiver.

I have seen investigators who spend so much time and effort on one case. When the case is either lost in a jury trial or never charged in the first place, they are devastated and give up the entire investigative effort.

So be wise in you investigation. Ensure you have vision and take care to always do the right thing. Track the crimes that the leaders are responsible for and conduct factual investigations, and know the elements of the crime and prove them in court beyond a reasonable doubt. Look at their finances and ensure you have resources investigating their money for forfeiture. Find their vulnerabilities and target them; roll their members and associates and make them cooperating witnesses and informants.

The outline presented in this book is meant to be a guide of things that you may wish to explore in conducting an investigation into a criminal enterprise. I have used these techniques effectively investigating criminal matters: targeting terrorist cells overseas and reducing risks in the private sector.

Make no mistake; the work is hard but it is also very rewarding. You will be accomplishing things in real life that they make movie and TV series about, be proud.

21

Prosecution

Throughout this book, I have written from the FBI or lead investigator perspective, and I will continue to do so in this chapter as well.

I am not an attorney. I would not be qualified to speak to the daily inner workings of federal, state, or local court proceedings.

I will speak to my expertise that was as the FBI case agent in dozens of federal cases that went to trial in federal court over my 25-year career.

I have also testified in state and local court on numerous occasions; however, for purpose of this publication, I will concentrate on the federal court.

I am focusing on the federal court system for two reasons; the first and the most important is the RICO and VICAR statutes are prosecuted in federal court. Second, if you have a task force with state and local police departments, it is unlikely they have brought their cases through the federal court system or testified in federal court. They will need training and guidance upfront to alleviate frustration on their part and on the part of the assigned AUSA.

On a side note, as long as the task force officers are willing and capable, there is no reason why they should not be assigned the lead on individual RICO cases as part of the investigation. To split the cases between investigators along jurisdictional lines, federal agents keeping all the federal cases and state and local officers taking all the local prosecutions, is possible, but it could be divisive to the task force. That is something that should be discussed with the task force officers and their executives. It can be done either way.

One of the advantages to a formal federal task force is the state and local police officers are sworn in as federal officers by the U.S. Marshals

Service. Once deputized and sworn in, they receive credentials and have federal arrest powers. Some of the state and local task force officers will be eager to assume the responsibility as the case agent on the RICO or VICAR investigations. Some will be resistant. Evaluate your own task force and make appropriate assignments based upon factual conclusions of that evaluation.

Whether the task force officers assume the role of case agent or not, they may be called to testify in federal court on the cases that the task force investigates. They also will be called upon to assist in trial preparation.

There is a difference in experience levels of task force officers as far as investigative procedures, prosecutive responsibilities, and testimony in court. In most state or local law enforcement agencies, the initial response is done by the patrol officer who writes a report. The report is reviewed and assigned to a detective who may have never responded to the initial crime scene. The detective investigates the crime, conducts interviews, and pulls together evidence to charge any person(s) responsible. Once the detective arrests the person(s), the evidence indicates that the person(s) committed the crime; the case is assigned to a district attorney investigator who gathers all the evidence and prepares for trial.

In the federal court system, the primary investigative agency will be responsible for all phase of the investigation, including preparation for trial.

As an FBI agent, I would respond to the initial crime scene and conduct interviews or collect evidence. I would then follow up on any leads and conduct the proper investigation. On one occasion, we identified a subject responsible for the crime I would continue the investigation, reviewing any pertinent criminal statutes. I would identify the elements of the crime that I thought the subject could be charged with and consulted with the AUSA.

Once the AUSA decided what charges would be brought against the subject, we would prepare the case for a grand jury indictment. The federal grand jury is a panel of 23 citizens who serve a set period and hear evidence presented by the government. They then vote to either charge (true bill) or not charge (no bill) the subject of the investigation.

Preparation for the grand jury usually called for additional investigation. As the case agent, I would be responsible for the grand jury preparation. I would also testify in front of the grand jury, presenting the case for the jurors review and return of a true bill (indictment). The true bill was the official document charging the subject of the investigation.

Once the case was indicted, I would prepare and oversee the arrest of the subject, unless the subject(s) was already in custody. Once the subjects are arrested they are brought before the U.S. Magistrate, for an initial appearance. During the initial appearance hearing, the subject is usually mandated into the custody of the U.S. Marshals. Depending on the severity of the charges and criminal history of the subject, the subject could be detained and a trial date would be set. The trial date may come quickly.

Preparation for trial in federal court is a tedious and labor-intensive enterprise. Even if your investigation is sound and evidence gathered to the elements of the crime are enough to convict the subject(s) beyond any doubt whatsoever, the defense attorneys will do everything in their power to cast that doubt on any aspect of your investigation.

Prior to trial, there will be evidence suppression hearings, detention hearings, and venue hearings. So, even the most ironclad case will be under the scrutiny of several defense attorneys and their investigators. Believe me when I say that every piece of evidence will be examined for appropriate collection and handling. Any piece of evidence that was not initialed and dated according to procedure will be questioned as to its authenticity.

You and your task force members may be verbally assaulted by defense attorneys during these pretrial hearings and during trial. The defense attorneys will make an attempt to make you look like an incompetent boob, indicating that you only caught their client because you couldn't catch the real culprit. Remember, that is their job. They aren't attacking you personally. Maintain your perspective and demeanor when testifying in these situations.

With all the preliminary hearings concluded, if your subject(s) haven't pleaded guilty, the real work will begin. When the trial date finally comes, you will be prepared more than you could have believed six months prior to trial.

In preparation for trial, the AUSA will want to interview every witness that will be called for the prosecution. The AUSA will have the investigative and police reports and will prepare questions for each witness crucial for the trial. It will be your job to ensure that either the witnesses are brought to the AUSA or you bring the AUSA to them. It all depends on the AUSA, and I have seen it both ways, sometimes a mixture of the two.

Of course, if some of the witnesses are in custody or in prison, you and the AUSA will have to go to them.

These witness interviews can be very delicate. The last thing you and the AUSA want to do is anger a witness through rude or arrogant behavior.

Put yourself in their position. The insider cooperating witnesses doesn't want to face their former partners in crime in court. Some victims are terrified of their attackers and will not want to see them in court (or anywhere). The witness is not a piece of evidence. Even criminals are still human beings. They must be treated with empathy and understanding.

Once trial starts, the investigation does not end. Have a couple of task force members available to cover any leads that may arise during trial. If the defense calls witnesses, run them for criminal histories. Identify yourself and ask them if they mind talking to you. Remember they don't have to talk to you; if they refuse to talk, act professionally, thank them, and walk away.

However, I can guarantee they won't talk to you if you don't ask. I have gathered valuable information by talking to the defense witnesses and assisted the AUSA in preparation for their testimony.

As the case agent, you may be called to testify in trial. It can be nerve wracking for the first couple of times, but as you gain experience, it can be extremely rewarding. Most defense attorneys know that an experienced federal case agent knows everything about the case. If given the opportunity, the case agent will tell the judge and jury just how guilty their client is, in detail. So the defense attorneys do not want to ask too many questions that would allow the agent to lay out the whole case again. Still, I have had defense attorneys that have allowed me to give synopsis of the case and evidence against their client. When testifying, I learned to watch for the "open door," an opportunity to lay out the evidence in a concise synopsis.

The best advice I can give to anyone testifying for the first couple of times is to start with a professional appearance. Get a haircut, shave, and wear your best suit. You may be the only federal agent or task force officer the jurors ever meet, so make a favorable impression.

When the defense attorney starts asking you questions, listen to the defense's question, take a second, and then answer the question. Pausing while you are thinking of your answer gives the AUSA a second to object if the question is inappropriate. Do not volunteer information that isn't in the question. The defense may be leading you down a path in their favor. Unless you are confident that the door is open to present evidence of the defendant's guilt, just answer their question. But be sure of your evidence and that you are comfortable with laying out the case or you may have to live with the consequences.

When you are asked questions look at attorney (AUSA and defense), but when you answer the questions look at the jurors—an important point to courtroom demeanor. Be confident and look into their eyes. Answer slowly but confidently. It is your case and you have done a good job investigating it. Show the jurors, judge, and everyone in the courtroom the evidence your task force gathered. Lay out how they proved beyond a reasonable doubt the elements of the crime that the defendant committed; be factual and concise.

If they believe you, you will see the jurors nodding their heads and smiling at you. If not, they will glare at you, and you will get a feeling for their negative demeanor. Your job is to tell the truth and represent the facts as a representative of the U.S. government.

Once the jury comes back and convicts (or God forbid acquits) your defendant, be professional, no high fives or NFL showboat dance. You did what you get paid for, so maintain professional demeanor. Save the celebration for later; get the task force together and celebrate a job well done. Start getting ready for the next trial. Keep going through the disruption and dismantlement phases. Trials and pretrial preparation should be a constant throughout the entire investigation.

22

Dismantlement

Whether the investigative techniques you decide to utilize are overt or covert. In fact, regardless of the investigative techniques your task force use during the course of the investigation, always remember the goal: dismantlement of the targeted criminal enterprise.

Utilize RICO and VICAR charges on leaders and mid-level managers of the enterprise to dismantle their activities and operations. You need to put the leaders and their successors in jail for a very long time. Once the organization is ineffective and cannot sustain daily operations, you will have met your goal; that is, the effective dismantlement of the criminal enterprise.

Trust me. Mission focus is a leadership trait that calls for a clear vision and a dogged determination. It is all too easy to get caught up in street crime enforcement. The street enforcement is meant to disrupt the organization's daily operations. Don't allow overzealous task force members to make street enforcement the focus of the investigation.

Street-level enforcement is understood by the local law enforcement agencies. It is also a lot of fun. Running around arresting those who thought they were protected by a criminal enterprise only to be snatched up by a federal task force was a great feeling. I know from firsthand experience. The NLR street-enforcement cases were akin to being "Batman." It would have been all too easy to just continue with the street-level enforcement and forget about the RICO case.

This is an all familiar trap that must be avoided. Executives from the local departments love to hear how many people were arrested this week. They will begin to track these statistics like the generals did body counts in the Vietnam War.

The dismantlement mission must be reviewed and emphasized at every task force meeting. Progress on the RICO and VICAR charges must be communicated at every chance to engage the leadership staff of the task force in the dismantlement mission. You will know when executives are engaged. They will begin to ask the status of the RICO case. The overall mission of dismantlement should be communicated and adopted by all the management of the task force agencies.

Please keep in mind the scope of the mission that you undertake from the onset of the investigation. Be realistic in your goals. Communicate effectively.

Taking on a mission "to dismantle the Italian Mafia" is not a practical goal for one task force. Targeting a vast and international criminal entity is the goal of a law enforcement agency such as the FBI. The FBI does so through a strategic overview and by the implementation of many task forces. A specific task force should set the goals to target a major branch of a criminal entity.

A good analogy is, "by chopping of branches of a tree, the tree will eventually die." The individual task forces concentrate on criminal enterprises and dismantle the branches to be of no use to the criminal entity, thus affecting the entire criminal entity, such as the Italian Mafia.

By setting realistic goals—goals that are measurable and attainable—the progress of the task force can be monitored and its success can be tracked. There are many task forces that start with lofty goals and objectives but lose focus and concentrate their efforts on arresting low-level criminals.

Losing focus causes these task forces to not being as effective as one that maintains its focus and attention on the dismantlement of the targeted criminal enterprise.

Section IV

Conclusion

23

Warnings/Cautions

Imagine that it is the end of the investigation, and for the past three years you and your task force have been disrupting the daily activities of the targeted criminal enterprise.

The criminal enterprise had conducted shootings, assaults, and murders, which were charged in the indictments. The leaders were all hardened criminals.

The AUSA has just returned indictments on 12 of the leaders of the criminal enterprise. The task force conducted arrest and search warrants on the RICO subjects, including 10 other major players in the criminal enterprise.

The multiagency takedown involved hundreds of police officers and agents from the region. The takedown went off without any major hitches. The case made the national news and the heads of the departments on the task force are full of praise for the efforts of the task force members. Conversely, within a month of the takedown, there is an increase in shootings and murders in the city.

Everyone is shocked. What the hell is going on?

One of the laws of physics is for every action, there is an equal and opposite reaction. There will be consequences as the result of your dismantlement of a powerful regional criminal enterprise.

Watch and evaluate the consequences of taking out a large gang or organization concentrated in an area of your city. The criminal enterprise that you dismantled may have been strong enough to keep a regional peace in their portion of a city.

As a result of the arrests and incarceration of the members of the criminal enterprise and the vacuum created by your task force, violence may spike in your city, as rival gangs fight for control of the vacated area.

Just be aware of the consequences of your actions and plan accordingly. Over the course of your investigation and certainly as you are planning the final takedown of the targeted criminal enterprise, look to other criminal enterprises of crews that may attempt to fill the power vacuum. Come down on them quickly and fill the power vacuum with your task force.

There is another and separate lesson that I learned in the NLR case. We accomplished our objectives and dismantled the NLR as a major presence in California.

In 2003, we convicted 13 leaders of the NLR. We had them shipped to federal prisons across the United States. The reasoning was we were sending them away from their power base, which was the state prison system in California.

However, by 2006, one of their leaders who was sentenced to 22 years and was serving his sentence in Beaumont Federal Prison in Texas was known to have recruited several federal white inmates to form a hybrid of the NLR. The Federal Bureau of Prisons confirmed an increase in the number of inmates that had affiliation with the NLR or the new NLR offshoot organization.

Results of our investigation showed that we did indeed dismantle the power base of the NLR in California. But we also took a dozen leaders of the NLR and spread them across the United States. Now it appears the NLR was growing in the federal prison system.

Don't get me wrong. I am not saying that you shouldn't investigate a criminal enterprise that has a major presence in your territory. I just want you to be aware there may be unsuspected consequences to your efforts. Not all of them will be what you had hoped for when you started the investigation.

24

Terrorist Organizations

In the fall of 2007, while serving in Iraq as the second in command of the FBI contingent, the FBI called on to assist the Department of Defense personnel in the identification and dismantlement of criminal and terror-related enterprises throughout the Iraqi theater of operations. We applied the principles of the criminal enterprise theory of investigation to the mission with some success.

From the start, we noticed a need for training of U.S. Military personnel in effective methods of the investigation of criminal enterprises to target the adversaries in Iraq. The soldiers conducting raids to gather intelligence were not versed in the basic principles of criminal investigation or intelligence collection.

For example, when conducting an operation to collect intelligence on a site, the military persons would gather papers, computers, ledgers, financial data, and anything they thought was intelligence for a raid location. They would throw it all in a bag and bring it back to the base for evaluation. When we asked where a crucial piece of intelligence was found and who was in the room linked to the intelligence, they could not answer.

To address this problem, the FBI developed ad hoc evidence collection techniques and taught them to the military personnel. Quick reference guides were prepared and given to the military personnel for reference. The training that we developed was well received and proved beneficial to the U.S. government's overall mission in Iraq.

At that time, we did what we could with the military forces that were deployed with us. However, there was no formal training program for U.S. Military personnel regarding the criminal/terrorist enterprise investigation.

We had suggested the current and future worldwide terrorism threat requires the United States to develop special operations forces and expand their expertise to include a sophisticated understanding of enterprise investigation techniques. These enhancements would include the proper identification and collection of evidence, development of sources, and the ability to quickly recognize and act on developing investigative leads.

We also proposed that the Department of Defense develop a pilot program to train a selected special operations forces unit on the theory of criminal enterprise investigation. Training would include investigative field techniques to advance the development and coordination of intelligence from any field of operation in the world to ensure critical evidence and information is understood and properly preserved for appropriate use.

The methods in the criminal theory of enterprise investigation included interviewing/interrogation, evidence collection and handling, mapping of enterprise leadership and methods/operations, informant development, and effective development and execution of actionable intelligence leading to the disruption/dismantlement of the enterprise an effective organization.

These methods proved very effective for the FBI in targeting and dismantlement of organized crime groups. These techniques have also been leveraged against domestic and international terrorist organizations.

The strength of utilizing the enterprise investigations method is the task force members are engaged to a level of expertise unrivaled by any action arm that is not a member of the task force.

For example, once trained on the criminal theory of enterprise investigation, the special operations forces unit would focus its attention on a specific threat. The trained unit would become the assigned operational arm for U.S. government intelligence efforts regarding the leadership of their specific assignment.

With the enhanced investigative capabilities and partnership (hopefully the formation of a task force) with intelligence agencies, such as the CIA, FBI, DIA, and Homeland Security, the trained unit would become experts on their assigned terrorist cell. This effort could also include foreign government law enforcement and military personnel. The task force would become well informed about their cell's leadership, methods, and operations.

The investigative enhancement is anticipated to allow them to investigate and draw educated conclusions on the terrorist cell during crucial operations, thereby maximizing time in hostile environments. They would develop the capability to understand the value of intelligence when they saw it during their limited time on scene in hostile environments.

The knowledgeable operators would quickly analyze and seize evidence crucial to the investigation while on scene. They would bring analytical expertise to the battle zone and be more informed while in the theater.

It is my opinion that applying the criminal enterprise theory of investigation and task force concept to specific terror cells would have a great positive impact in our international counterterrorism efforts.

25

Private Industry Applications

As I transitioned to private security from the FBI, I found many of the intelligence, analytical, and critical thinking skills, which I had learned and utilized to dismantle criminal and terrorist organizations, could be applied to the private sector.

Existing companies are going to have external, internal, and industry threats generic to their organization. The skills that I learned investigating cases in the FBI provided me with the tools to examine a company's vulnerabilities. Once the weaknesses are uncovered, the skills assisted me in developing plans to circumvent risks due to vulnerabilities.

My first job outside the FBI was as the physical security leader at an electrical transmission only utility company in the midwest. It was imperative to assess the existing security program before launching an in-house intelligence-based security function. The assessment was the first step in the utilization of the intelligence skills I had attained as an FBI agent.

I had to determine whether current personnel were capable and willing to initiate and maintain the intelligence function. I also had to convince senior management of the value of an intelligence program. Without adequate resources and support, the new program would fail.

The initial analysis of the utility's security program revealed the security department was deficient in several key components. There was a lack of focus, organization, vision, leadership, structure, and discipline.

There was no central repository of written standard operating procedures to guide even the simplest of duties within the department. To address this problem, I directed the department to compile a manual of operations. This served as a central repository that documented and organized security policies, procedures, and processes for the reference of all company personnel, not just security.

In addition, the individual security personnel worked on separate projects and failed to share them with the rest of the team, leading to an overall lack of focus. Security specialists neglected to write reports or document security incidents. Where necessary, security staff received formal training on aspects of their jobs.

With the stabilization of basic security duties, we launched into the intelligence-based initiatives. We found that the development of an effective intelligence program allowed our organization to identify, track, and minimize damage by known adversaries along with the potential adversaries' intent and capabilities.

Examples of types of threats evaluated and tracked were insider threats, external threat (specific to our organization), industry threats (specific to our industry), regional threats, national threats, and international threats.

The ancient but applicable Sun Tzu's *Art of War* axiom, "Know your Enemy and know yourself and you can fight a thousand battles without disaster," still applies today.

Do you know and track your real or potential adversaries? How can you protect your organization if you don't know where you are vulnerable to be attacked from internal or external forces?

The key is a simple concept; evaluate your security department, and ask yourself are your people capable of implementing an intelligence-based security posture? In addition, determine if you management is supportive, are they educated on the benefits of properly gathered, analyzed, and actioned intelligence information?

After you garner executive management support and ensure you have a skilled security staff, the first step to an intelligence-based security program is an enterprise-wide assessment. This assessment is of the organization and is separate of the initial assessment you conducted of the security department.

Generally, the enterprise-wide assessment is designed to evaluate your organization and what you need to protect. This is done by identifying threats and their capability to bring harm to your organization. Simple questions for the base assessment are as follows: Who has made threats to harm your company? What is their capability? How vulnerable is your organization to be attacked? How can the company to be attacked? What is the probability of the attack? What is your risk? Finally, what are you going to recommend for mitigating and reducing that risk?

Intelligence-based security is a fact-based decision that you make by determining an acceptable level of risk based upon a comprehensive assessment of all threats, vulnerabilities, and risks.

Many companies close their eyes and pray that nothing adverse ever happens to their company or organization.

Let me sum it up for you. How many times in your life have you or a member of a team said, "If only we had known that yesterday...?" Well, the advantage of a robust intelligence program is the information you develop through the assessment, evaluation, analysis, and mitigation techniques as part of that program that will assist you in strategic and tactical planning. You may actually recognize what is coming and prepare appropriately for the adversity.

You will have enough information to make a more informed decision and prevent the number of times you discover critical facts after the incident.

I am a "true believer" and want you to succeed. I am confident the more people who see the advantages of an intelligence-based security posture in private security, the more we can protect the people and assets entrusted to us in our critical but often forsaken role as security professionals.

The future of private security will depend on security professionals who enhance their departments by conducting analysis of past incidents, law enforcement records, demographics, crime statistics, industry history, presence of criminal and/or terrorist organizations, direct external threats, internal threats along with evaluating present security operations to propose cost-efficient security improvements to provide satisfactory levels of risk acceptance to the evaluated enterprise.

As detailed throughout this work, the advantages of knowing who your adversary is and what capabilities he/she has to bring to bear against your organization allows you to plan and prepare accordingly.

The principle of intelligence-based security is to train organizations to develop sufficient situational awareness to determine who has the intent of harming the organization. Start by asking these questions: Who is your potential adversary? Do they have the intent to harm your organization? How do you know that they wish to harm your organization? What is his/her/their capability to carry out the threat to harm you? Where are you vulnerable? How could anyone harm your organization if they wanted to do so?

Tracking threats and vulnerabilities specific to your organization is the key to minimize risk and damage that may be caused in any attack.

153

For example, once an attack on your organization occurs, having a list of subjects who are capable of such an attack and have the intent to harm your organization is a critical component of the intelligence program. Possessing the ability to quickly turn over a list of known subjects to appropriate law enforcement officials may be the difference between one or two attacks or a multitude of devastating attacks severely affecting your operations.

To ensure clarity, the following paragraphs will define terms such as threat and vulnerability as described in this context.

The word "threat" being defined as a person or organization that may possess the capability and intent to cause harm to any entity it finds "offensive" or believes may have wronged the person defined as the "threat" in some manner.

An important point is that a potential threat may have the capability to attack an entity, but without intent, the entity will not be attacked.

A good example is the information technology manager in any company, who has the capability to sabotage the organization's computer systems through deliberate attacks on the hardware and software, but as a trusted employee we expect the IT manager to protect those systems, not damage them.

Nevertheless, if the IT manager develops malicious intent to harm the organization because of problems with his/her boss, the results of an insider attack could be devastating.

A threat may have high intent to attack an entity, but if it does not possess the capability, any attack will be ineffective until the threat devotes the time and resources to develop the capability to carry out an attack. This gives the threatened entity time to monitor the threat's capability and prepare for any attack as the threat's capability increases.

Of the two groups, any group or person who is being evaluated as a threat that has a high capability to carry an attack, but no immediate intent, must be a higher priority than the determined incapable attacker. It takes time and resources to develop capability, but intent can be developed in a matter of minutes, even seconds.

Moreover, a threat with capability may attack an entity as an ancillary target, for example, if a group of criminals decide to rob a bank. They may attempt to cut power and communications by attacking an electrical utility substation and fiber-optic communications vault. The power or communications company may not be the direct target, but the consequences of any ancillary attack could still be devastating to critical infrastructure.

The word "vulnerability" is defined as the evaluation of the entity assets and determination of susceptibility of those assets to an attack. An entity may be an ancillary target of a threat; any vulnerability assessment should include developing security protections to ensure sustained operations of the evaluated entity.

As you evaluate the specific and general threats that have developed the intent and have the capability to attack you, you must evaluate your assets to determine how vulnerable your assets are to an attack.

For example, chain link fences and padlocks on a remote unmanned location without any means to receive alarms, monitor alarms, or any camera systems to view the location is more vulnerable than a manned site with analytic video camera systems monitored by a 24-hour central alarm station.

The key questions for the vulnerability assessment component are as follows: What are we going to protect? How are we protected now? How would we attack our organization? How can risk to operations be minimized?

Vulnerability assessments of critical assets cross the human factor but must include the possibility of harm from weather events or natural disasters. The critical asset must be looked at from every angle, human and nature, for protection.

My security experience includes the following specific examples of where we applied the intelligence-based security techniques to real-world situations.

There was a problem with criminals that were cutting holes in the perimeter fencing and stealing copper grounding clamps and wire to sell as scrap.

There was also an issue with people shooting up the wooden structures that supported the power lines. These were criminal activities that called for evaluation, analysis, and investigation. They were opportunities that were right in my wheel house.

BLENDED SECURITY

Another area that I noticed in the private security world was the silos that existed between the several departments responsible for security. The cyber security, physical security, compliance department, and risk management rarely coordinated their security efforts with each other. There was no overview of threats that may spill across the entire enterprise. The physical security department may receive threats, but any threat received is analyzed from the Physical Security perspective.

Who was to say if the threat possessed a cyber capability if the cyber security department never even heard of the guy? There were no regular meetings between security departments to analyze, evaluate, and prioritize threats.

Throughout my law enforcement and security career, of more than 30 years, one of the areas that was the most difficult to overcome but very crucial to success was the need for collaboration between diverse departments with varying missions and viewpoints.

For example, U.S. federal agents, state and local law enforcement may be investigating the same gang in their respective jurisdictions but looking at the gang from different angles. The local law enforcement officer wants the gang out of their city. If the gang moves to the next city over, their problem is solved. The state officer's mission is to clear their state of the gang. The federal agent, however, has the mission to disrupt and dismantle the gang's operations and membership. The federal agencies concentrate much of their criminal enterprise investigations on bringing the different agencies into a task force with the overall mission to dismantle the gang.

Using the different federal, state, and local methods to target the gang's activities in a collaborative effort maximizes the effectiveness of all levels of law enforcement. The collaborative law enforcement task force has proved to be a successful tool to target gangs in the United States.

It is becoming more and more apparent that in the modern world and current threat environment, that all levels of security, physical security, information security, cyber security, and risk management personnel must also coordinate their efforts dealing in threats that cross all security arenas.

As in the law enforcement example, each of the security departments in an organization has its own area of responsibility, or their specific mission. The physical security professional will focus on the physical protection of personnel and assets. The information security professional focuses on the protection of an entity's information. The cyber security professional concentrates on the protection of information technology systems.

Even though there is some crossover of their specific missions, these departments rarely meet unless there is a crisis. During a crisis, it is often too late to prevent substantial damage.

As the physical security leader at a medium-sized company, I initiated and led such a task force to address insider threats. Representing physical security, I engaged personnel from cyber security, information assurance, human resources, and legal department.

We met once a month and discussed any internal issues that arose; we ensured the protection of employees' rights, but we also reduced risk to the company by placing tripwires in the IT systems. If the employee resolved their issues, the team removed the tripwires. However, if the employee made attempts to harm the company, we were notified through the placement of the tripwires and took action before any malicious act could be completed.

The program was successful because of the collaborative efforts of the diverse team members working with the common goal of defending the company while respecting the rights of the employees.

The theme is to examine the formation of a security task force to address any threats specific to a company or organization. The task force should work together to leverage their different but valuable perspectives to each threat. Each threat should be analyzed, evaluated, and the risk be mitigated by this collaborative team. Physical and cyber security personnel should examine the threat stream through their varying perspectives, but for a common cause, protect the company from the threat.

Upon formation of a security task force, physical and cyber security personnel should evaluate the possibility of developing collaborative assessment tools and in the future developing collaborative incident response plans.

Assess and defend against the cyber-led attack that defeats physical security measures or the physical-led attack designed to gain access to cyber assets.

The analysis of the threat stream should include but not be limited to the following threats: insider threats described as disgruntled employee/contractor. External threat described as terrorists, disgruntled customer, or organized lone wolf, and finally, state-sponsored attacks.

The common security mission should include the prevention of a coordinated attack (physical and cyber). A coordinated effort attacking both physical and cyber systems should be of great concern.

The goal of security efforts must include the collaboration of all security elements in a company to assess and defend against the cyber-led attack that defeats company physical security measures or the physical-led attack designed to gain access to company cyber assets.

The security task force should conduct a collaborative assessment of existing threats. In any initial threat assessments, some questions that security professionals should be able to answer regarding their own company are as follows: Who is my biggest threat? What is their capability? Physical capability? Cyber capability? How are we defending against them? Document the threats and monitor their activities, and then develop and implement measures to reduce risk based upon threat capabilities.

Knowing your adversary and your organization's vulnerabilities is the key to reduce risk to company personnel and assets. The formation and effective operation of a blended security task force can strengthen your security posture through the collaborative efforts of diverse viewpoints on a common problem.

Another advantage to the collaborative group meeting regularly is that they know each other and their roles well, and in a crisis can react quickly to the developing situation. It is difficult to form a collaborative security group when the crisis hits. Working together as a team on a regular basis can smooth out the kinks in the team and assist in emergency operations.

Meeting on a regular basis can help your organization see through the fog of battle when critical thinking is key. The formation of a blended security task force should be included in emergency management planning and operations, but meeting regularly on routine security threats will strengthen the bond between them.

Teamwork with the best interests of the organization must be paramount.

26

Practical Application

Let's conduct a practical exercise. We can use the techniques illustrated in this book to evaluate, analyze, and address a current crime problem in rest of the Wisconsin. Wisconsin and the entire United States are currently experiencing a problem with heroin addiction.

The first step is to identify the crime problem. Heroin use isn't new; it has been around for some time. Nevertheless, heroin use in the middle class has dramatically increased in the past decade. It is no longer hidden in the back streets and alleys of the city's downtrodden areas. On a weekly basis, media in Wisconsin reports on the "heroin epidemic" in central and southeastern Wisconsin.

Media attention has increased along with the number of deaths due to heroin overdoses. According to the state Department of Health Services, there were 187 deaths in 2012, nearly thrice as much as those (67 people) who died of heroin overdose in 2008. The public is aware there is a problem. The politicians demand something be done about the problem and law enforcement is looked upon to handle the problem.

So, continuing with the heroin crime problem in Wisconsin, what do we do as law enforcement to address the problem? We gather the basic intelligence and conduct an assessment.

What kind of heroin is prevalent? Through open source and official reporting, we find it to be "black tar" heroin. DEA has verified this information in a report they composed in 2015.

Since the black tar heroin has been identified in Wisconsin, and the source of black tar heroin is Mexico, an educated assumption can be made that Mexican cartels are involved at some level in the Wisconsin heroin crime problem. With the Mexican cartels involved there will be an involved interstate and international aspect to the investigation.

Oftentimes, there are varying jurisdictional levels to a crime problem. In the example of the heroin problem, local law enforcement will address the level in their jurisdiction usually street-level pushers and low-level distributors. These subjects are plentiful, and the local department can show results through numerous arrests, but they are easy for the criminal enterprise to replace.

These subjects rarely know middle or upper level cartel connections and are generally not worthy as top-level informants, as they are usually users themselves and not dependable.

So, in order to get to the root of the problem and interdict the heroin flow to Wisconsin, it is recommended that U.S. federal agents target the middle and upper management of the Mexican cartel responsible for moving drugs to the U.S. midwest and Milwaukee, Wisconsin, in particular. This is where our subject and potential informant base will be, middle level criminal enterprise members.

Next, let's identify who should be the law enforcement agencies we gather to address the problem. The agencies we would want to contact to form a working group.

The responsibility for the heroin problem–related crimes crosses several jurisdictions. The intent here is to give the reader an overview of law enforcement roles in major investigations.

The federal agencies that would have jurisdiction and would be considered as primary partners in the working group would be the FBI. The FBI would investigate which criminal organizations are trafficking heroin. They also would investigate what other crimes they are involved in on an interstate or international level.

The DEA has primary investigative responsibility for narcotics trafficking.

The ATF investigates firearms violations.

The U.S. Postal Office may also have an investigative interest as major cartels may use the postal service to launder and ship money.

If investigation shows an avenue into the U.S. Military, the U.S. Army's Criminal Investigations Division, and the U.S. Navy's Naval Criminal Investigative Service may be interested in joining the working group as primary or secondary partners.

Immigration and Naturalization Service (INS) would be a good secondary partner because of the revelation that Mexican Cartels are involved in heroin trafficking.

The U.S. Probation Office can be a great ancillary partner to any law enforcement working group, as the investigation progresses and subjects are identified that may be on federal probation.

The Internal Revenue Service is also a valuable asset to investigate tax evasion charges on enterprise leaders.

Initial coordination between federal agencies when addressing a new crime problem is vital. Although investigation into the heroin crime problem may be new to Wisconsin, any of the above-mentioned federal agencies may have ongoing investigations on the criminal enterprise that may be bringing heroin to Wisconsin. They could have critical historical information on the group you will be investigating, and coordination with the investigators in other ongoing investigations will be critical in the initial assessment.

This coordination also ensures any politics that may come into play at an early stage and at least give you the awareness of who is investigating what criminal enterprise through coordination with federal agency headquarters elements.

On the prosecution side, the U.S. Attorney's Offices in Madison and Milwaukee would require coordination, as there are two federal judicial districts in Wisconsin.

So, let's come back to our heroin crime problem. There is a HIDTA in Milwaukee. A good place to start and gather intelligence on heroin trafficking is the Great Lakes Region. The HIDTA has a myriad of drug-related crime problems, and although they will share information with you, they will not specifically target the heroin issue. So, it is decided to form a working group specific to the heroin problem.

Let's say for the sake of argument and because of my own background that the FBI takes the lead, the DEA, ATF, and INS decide to dedicate an agent to the working group, and U.S. Probation will be available on an on-call basis. The U.S. Military wants to stay informed but can't dedicate any resources to the Wisconsin-based working group. The Western District of Wisconsin U.S. Attorney's Office in Madison has dedicated and assigned an AUSA to the case and coordinated with the Eastern District of Wisconsin to ensure de-confliction.

The next step is to examine what state, county, and local law enforcement agencies have jurisdiction and may wish to be involved in the heroin working group. The goal is to form a working group that will eventually be formalized into an Organized Crime and Drug Enforcement Task Force (OCDETF) investigative proposal.

The State of Wisconsin has a statewide investigative agency under the Department of Justice, and the Division of Criminal Investigation (DCI) has the capability to become a primary member of the heroin working group.

The Wisconsin DOJ also oversees the Wisconsin Statewide Intelligence Center (WISC), a potential intelligence resource for the heroin task force. Explore obtaining a WISC analyst dedicated to the heroin problem from the state.

The Wisconsin State Patrol should be briefed on the existence of the heroin working group and would be a valuable ancillary member, especially for any task force that may have the need for a traffic stops, surveillance, or support in and around any freeways in the state.

The major police and sheriff's departments in the largest metropolitan cities, in this case, are the Milwaukee and Madison Police Departments. Milwaukee and Dane County Sheriff's Departments should be solicited for primary membership to the heroin task force.

The crime problem is certainly prevalent in the large cities, but in this case, it also extends into many of the middle class and wealthy suburbs.

So, ensure as the crime problem is analyzed in the suburbs and that agencies with significant heroin issues are either included as members of the heroin task force or are informed of the progress of the investigation.

This move is not altogether altruistic; subjects, informants, and intelligence can and will be gleaned from all the avenues addressed here, not just the large cities.

Ensure all law enforcement contacts are treated with dignity and respect; you never know when you may need to call them again.

In addition, because of political under tows, the major police departments may not join the heroin task force. Many large police departments do not desire to participate in FBI or DEA task forces, as the federal agencies are the lead agencies and the major police departments want to lead and not follow the "feds." So, manpower for the heroin task force may indeed come from smaller police departments where one of two heroin deaths is a significant crime problem.

Besides the police, there are other agencies that must be contacted and briefed regarding the heroin task force. District attorneys' offices in the districts with primary law enforcement membership on the heroin task force should be briefed and even invited to add an assistant district attorney (ADA) to the heroin task force. The investigation will undoubtedly include state and local charges, and dedicated ADAs will ensure smooth prosecutive opinions and actions at the state and local levels. Ensure the assigned AUSA is included in meetings with the ADAs; lawyers talk a different language than law enforcement people. Give them the opportunity to get to know each other and do some "lawyer speak."

Besides the law enforcement and prosecutive arms of the heroin task force, there must be an honest effort to include community groups that may be involved in the heroin-related community, half-way houses, drug treatment centers, church groups, schools, and volunteers. They deal with heroin-related problems and must be contacted and briefed as to the goals of the heroin task force.

They will know the ins and outs of the local heroin problems. They can and will be a valuable intelligence resource in the future. They also want the same thing that law enforcement wants: reduction of the crime problem. Engage them honestly and do your best to form an alliance to address the crime problem.

OK, now we have our probable working group, which will be formalized into the heroin task force mapped out; the primary members agencies are the U.S. Attorney's Office in Madison, FBI, DEA, ATF, DCI, WISC (analyst), Milwaukee Police Department, Madison Police Department, Dane County Sheriff's, Milwaukee County Sheriff's, Middleton Police Department, Greenfield Police Department, and Oak Creek Police Department.

Primary members have dedicated at least one person full time to the heroin task force. They will reassign the majority of their other duties and report full time to an established off-site, dedicating their time to addressing the heroin problem in Wisconsin. The press has reported the formation of the heroin task force; your investigation will be overt.

Early on and throughout the investigation, evaluate the primary task force members for investigative proficiency. Provide training for those who need it and set up some team training to help members "gel."

The gathering, evaluating, and analyzing of intelligence in any investigation is vital and must remain a constant component throughout the investigation and into the prosecutive stages.

Mission focus must also remain constant. Once you define the crime problem, develop a general plan with a mission statement to address the crime problem. In this case, the mission statement can be as simple as "Thorough investigation and effective prosecution reduce and alleviate the heroin flow to Wisconsin. Reduce the number of heroin related deaths to half in the first year." A proven formula is the disruption of the criminal enterprise's daily operations: the trafficking of heroin, along with the identification and RICO prosecution of major heroin drug traffickers in Wisconsin. Develop and document a plan, without focus any working group or task force will drift like a rudderless ship.

The next steps are to continue the intelligence gathering efforts; the who, what, where, and when; and the real nuts and bolts of the investigation. Start out by identifying who is distributing heroin on your local streets. Get the WISC analyst with the HIDTA and FBI analysts. Begin an organizational chart of Mexican drug cartels in the Great Lakes Region. If there are any in Wisconsin, these will be your RICO targets. Vet out all information on the RICO targets. Investigation of these subjects will include information such as past arrests, court actions, financial information, and business and family contacts. Once you know them, get them in any way possible that you can.

In conjunction with the RICO effort to target leaders of any heroin trafficking network in Wisconsin, find the street-level dealers and start squeezing them. The main mission is to disrupt the cartel's daily operations, but always look for cooperating witnesses and/or informants. Those that have mid-level contacts should be recruited as informants.

Use the disruption and street-level operations to gather intelligence to identify vulnerabilities. For example, how money is getting from the street-level dealers to the Mexican cartel?

In Los Angeles, they would drive vehicles with the money in hidden compartments directly down to Mexico. They would also use small Mexican markets with check cashing facilities to wire the money down to Mexico. Do not rule out these techniques, but do not think these are the only methods for moving money. Do your homework. Work the streets, develop informants, identify weaknesses, and exploit them.

Continue the RICO investigation and the street-level disruption until you have successfully resolved the crime problem.

Realize that the first-wave subjects of RICO indictments will be replaced by the Mexican cartel to continue the heroin drug flow to Wisconsin. Be prepared to continue the investigation past the first wave.

Also be aware the criminals will evolve their activity based upon your investigation. You must have the intelligence capability to identify those evolutions and the investigative tools in place to address them. You must develop the ability to evolve when they do. With a crime problem like heroin, the investigations may go on for years.

27

End Game

The intent of this book is to provide an instructional guide to investigate a criminal enterprise. The end game was the dismantlement of the targeted criminal enterprise as an effective organization.

Criminals usually form a criminal enterprise to pool their resources and maximize their profits, while minimizing their risk of detection. Ironically, the formation of a task force and utilization of the criminal enterprise theory of investigation to target the criminal enterprise also pools limited law enforcement resources into a mission focused group.

The results of a well-led and successful task force are shared by all members involved. There is no better feeling than being part of a team that faced adversity, hardship, and danger together and prevailed when odds were against them. The bond that is formed by such a team are long lasting and rewarding.

Relish the team that you are forming and will work with for a number of years. They will hold your life in their hands when you go on raids.

I have learned through personal experience that applying these techniques to private sector security departments has proven to have the same team building reinforcements. I have been fortunate and privileged to have served in the law enforcement and security professions.

For me, it was an honor to defend the constitution and defend the weak, those that have no hope for personal safety except for law enforcement.

I will leave you with a training point that I always told new FBI agents as I was training them in the field. "Always do the right thing and never do anything illegal, unethical, or unsafe."

Be proud, be fair, and be safe.

28

War Stories

After all the textbook-type narrative tone in this book, I thought it might be worthwhile to add a chapter at the end that included some war stories from the NLR case. These are told from my point of view. I am sure there are other sides of the story. Others might even contest some of what I say here. If you want to hear the other side of the story, go read others book.

When I was in boot camp at Fort Leonard Wood in 1975, one of our drill sergeants told us: Do you know the difference between a war story and a fairy tale? A fairy tale starts out "Once upon a time" and a war story starts out "This ain't no shit."

OK, let's go with "this ain't no shit..."

INK

As I am weaving back and forth through traffic on the busy San Bernardino freeway at 80 miles an hour in my FBI Ford Crown Victoria, lights flashing and police sirens wailing, I am hyped up. Adrenaline is coursing through my body. Pushing the talk button on the car radio microphone, I am yelling louder than I had intended. I am calling on the Bureau radio for the two other younger FBI agents to back off and let the marked police units take the lead in the chase.

The other two agents are young and caught up in the heat of the moment. They are even more hyped up than I am. The subject we are chasing is wanted for a murder. He shot some guy with a shotgun. He blasted the other guy from one car to another over some bullshit argument. The guy is dangerous and we have been after him for about a month.

The shooter is supposed to be an NLR member or at least an associate. It is one of the first cases that we are working on together as a true task force, the NLR Task Force in Los Angeles, California.

It looks like the other FBI agents finally hear me on the radio. I see them slow their Bureau cars down, allowing two Fontana Police marked units and one California Highway Patrol unit to take the lead in the high speed pursuit. I see the target of our pursuit: a huge red 1970s Cadillac. We continue to barrel down the freeway at maddening speeds. Cars are swerving and beeping their horns at the Cadillac. The killer is leading a multijurisdictional parade of law enforcement vehicles who are trailing in pursuit.

As I drive my Crown Victoria mid-pack in the pursuit, I think back on how we got here, this warm, sunny California day.

I first heard about the guy we were chasing from Glenn Willet of the SSU. For purposes of this story, we will call him Ink. Ink had blasted and killed a guy with a shotgun for no apparent reason. The two of them got in an argument and the subject drove up alongside the victim's car and shot him with the shotgun while they were both moving down a Fontana side street. The Fontana Police Department obtained a local warrant for him for murder, and the NLR Task Force was looking for him but was having trouble finding him.

During that time, I wasn't working with the NLR Task Force. They were hooked up with DEA because they had thought the FBI was moving too slow. I was working independently with Glenn Willett and his buddy Ricky Hahn, a San Bernardino Sheriff's deputy. We had been working up cases on NLR guys on our own. I wanted to show the NLR Task Force what an experienced FBI agent could accomplish.

So, Glenn, Ricky, and I sat down in Glenn's office and pulled together all the information that we could on Ink. We pulled his criminal background and found the guy with several arrests and convictions. He had spent some time in California prisons. It was rumored that he was an NLR member or at least an associate.

The SSU evidence wasn't enough to validate Ink as an NLR member, but he had been reported as hanging with NLR members in and out of prison. We found out who his old cellmates were when he was in prison. We identified his friends, family, and associates. We gathered, evaluated, and prioritized every bit of intelligence that we could on Ink.

The next stage was an all-out push to locate and arrest Ink. We hit the streets hard, beating on doors and interviewing anyone that we thought would lead us to a good location for Ink. It was hard and exhausting work but we kept at it.

We were all experienced enough to know that you make your own luck. The more doors we knocked on and the more people that we talked to, the more likely it was that we would develop that one lead that would lead to Ink.

Soon word had gotten out that we were looking for Ink. Since the NLR Task Force was also looking for him, it wasn't long before I got a call from them.

They liked what Glenn, Ricky, and I were doing and asked if we could join forces in our search for Ink. I agreed and soon we were meeting together as a group.

We joined forces and compared notes. We then prioritized leads that could help in our search for Ink. For the next two weeks, we hit the streets as a team. There were many long nights knocking on doors of some of the most undesirable areas of Fontana, San Bernardino, Ontario, Rialto, and up in Victorville. We were hit anyone that knew or even heard of Ink.

We were also hitting NLR drug labs and NLR hangouts. I was using the Ink case as a "coming out party." We were letting them know that we were coming after the NLR as a group. Those two weeks that we searched for Ink were intense and sometimes nonstop, 24-hour days were common. The more we worked together, the closer we got as a working team. Over that period, the more we worked together, the more the group trusted and followed my lead.

Finally, in the afternoon of the second week, we got the break that we had been searching for weeks. We got information that Ink was staying with his auntie in Fontana at a trailer in a trailer court. We quickly set up at the trailer and watched it all night.

His car, which we knew was a red Cadillac, wasn't there so we didn't believe he was there. To conserve our resources, we decided to break down the Task Force into two shifts and surveil the trailer for a couple of days.

Since we had a Fontana officer on the NLR Task Force, he was responsible for coordination with the Fontana Police Department.

Our plan was simple, if Ink showed up and there were enough resources on-site, they would arrest him once he got out of the car. If the on-scene officers didn't feel safe, they would call for backup and the Fontana Police Department would send resources to assist the Task Force members in the arrest of Ink.

So, as things never go the way you want them to, Ink showed up about a half an hour after we spilt the Task Force. He drove his red Cadillac up to the trailer and was out of the car and in the trailer before the guys on scene could get him. They did see him. They verified it was Ink. They knew he was in the trailer.

They called the Fontana cops for back up and then called me. I had everyone on the Task Force respond back to the location.

Ink was still in the trailer when we all got there. I still liked the plan. We close on the trailer and box in his car once he came out of the trailer. Stop him before he got into the car.

However, the lieutenant from Fontana actually preferred Ink to get in his car. He wanted to do a traffic stop on him.

I strongly advised against this. I told him putting a wanted killer behind the wheel of the large Cadillac was as dangerous as handing him a gun.

We argued until he called the FBI supervisor who told me that since it was a local warrant out of Fontana that I should let them handle it the way they wanted. OK, thanks for having my back, which leads us back to the beginning of this particular war story, blazing down the freeway.

As we had planned with the Fontana cops, when Ink came out of the trailer, he loaded up in the Cadillac. The Fontana cops had a marked unit pull him over, which Ink did at first. We watched over the officer as he turned on his light and the red Cadillac eased over to the side of the road. Huh, maybe I was wrong.

But then as the Fontana officer opened his door to get out of his unit, Ink floored the accelerator on the powerful Cadillac. He took off like a bat out of hell. The chase was on.

Ink was driving like a mad man in the mid-morning southern California traffic. A parade of marked and unmarked cop cars started chasing him, matching his every move.

He started out on side streets, roaring through streets lined by stucco side houses. From the side streets, Ink made it to the Foothill Boulevard, a palm tree lined major thoroughfare. He was weaving in and out of traffic, with total regard for other drivers; he occasionally drove on the wrong side of the road.

Eventually, he made it to the San Bernardino freeway. Ink was still being followed by a static line of police cars, undercover, and FBI vehicles. All of us were trying to keep Ink in sight and close enough to arrest him if he bailed on his foot from the Cadillac. Ink was hitting triple digit speeds. At over 100 miles an hour, the chase was getting more dangerous all the time.

We provided NLR Task Force handheld radios to the Fontana Police, but they were calling out the chase on their own radios. We couldn't hear a damn thing, what they were saying or planning.

The task force guys were staying far enough behind the Fontana Police marked units and allowed them to work. Most of us from the task force were close enough to assist in any foot chase, if there was one. It was what we expected, sooner or later.

We had been chasing Ink for about 20 minutes when he got off the freeway. He was driving on the wrong side of a six-lane highway. The police followed him and we followed the police. The speeds were reaching 70 or 80 miles an hour on the highway.

Cars were trying to get out of the way, and there were several accidents as Ink banged off some of the cars in traffic.

The vehicle in pursuit again took to some side streets but in a more commercial area. We were zooming by businesses and restaurants at break neck speed. People were watching from the street in shocked awe.

Finally, Ink pulled into a hospital parking lot. I watched as several cars followed him but two of the marked units peeled off. I followed the parade into the parking lot.

The marked units that peeled off came across the NLR Task Force radio. They were going to try to block Ink's escape from the parking lot and set up a barricade with their cars. So, this was it. They were going to force Ink's hand and end the vehicle pursuit. I told our guys to let the uniformed cops take the lead but to ensure that Ink couldn't escape, at all costs.

Ink drove around the parking lot only one time before he entered a four-story cement parking structure on the edge of the hospital parking lot. The big Cadillac roared into the parking structure followed by a marked Fontana Unit, a couple of task force members, including another FBI agent, and then myself in my Crown Victoria.

I could see that Ink was going too fast. He couldn't make the turn on the second level. The Cadillac smashed into several parked cars. I remember seeing the rear end of the caddy popping up in the air and coming down with enough force to pop one of the rear tires. It popped as loud as a shotgun blast.

The crash stunned Ink for a moment. He didn't get out of the car right away. Many of us chasing him came out of their cars quickly. We were heading toward the crashed red Cadillac on foot with guns drawn. Just before any of us got to the car, Ink flung the door of the Cadillac open and burst out of the passenger door on foot.

We were on the second floor, about 15 feet above the ground. The parking structure was solid concrete and the space between the floors was open to the outside. It was not totally enclosed. Ink was running away from his car and toward the stairwell on the other side of the parking structure.

Well, as we were closing in on Ink, he could see some of us were going to beat him to the stairwell. I knew it too and was one of them that had taken a route to cut him off. I was ready for the arrest. I was watching his hands, watching for a gun. He was wearing a white dress shirt with the tails pulled out and a tee shirt underneath.

As we closed in from all sides, Ink stopped, but only for a second. He was running out of options. All these cops were closing in on him. Ink turned toward the concrete barrier that was open to the outside and put his hands out in front of his head, like a diver. He hesitated for a second and then Ink jumped headfirst off the second floor to the grass and concrete 15 feet below.

I was amazed. I ran up to the side of the building and saw Ink on the ground. He was staggering but he was getting up.

I turned to run to the stairwell, which was about 20 feet away. I paused for a second as I saw one of the Ontario Police officers from the NLR Task Force jump up on the edge of the concrete barrier and fly into space spread eagled like a sky diver or Spiderman.

If it would have been 20 years earlier, I might have followed him into the thin air, but as I was in my forties and with a surgically reconstructed right knee, I headed for the stairwell to run down the stairs. Discretion is the better part of valor.

The chase wasn't over. As far as I knew the Ontario officer was in a one-on-one fight with Ink, not good odds.

As I came out of the stairwell, I saw Ink sitting on his butt about 40 yards from the parking structure. The OPD officer was still running at him; he was closing in on him quickly. Another OPD Task Force officer was tracking Ink through the rifle sights of his M-16. He had steadied the rifle on the concrete edge of the concrete parking structure on the ground floor.

As we were running toward Ink, he reached inside of his shirt with his right hand. It looked like he was grabbing for something. I thought it might be a gun. I raised my gun, as did several other officers, but not more than 10 feet behind Ink and the OPD officer there was a preschool class of several five-year-old kids. The teacher had brought them out to play in the yard. They were lined up like little baby ducks behind their mother. If we started shooting, they would be in the line of fire. We all saw it and all of us showed restraint; we didn't fire on Ink.

A second later, the OPD officer who followed Ink off the second story reached him. He hit Ink in the head with an elbow, stunning him. The OPD officer was a ground fighting instructor; he had Ink on the ground in a flash. He was placing handcuffs on him as we all reached the scene.

We didn't find a gun on Ink. He had been reaching for a cigarette and a lighter. He was trying to get a final smoke in before he went to jail. That smoke almost got him killed. If those kids wouldn't have been there, I am sure Ink would have gotten shot, mostly because I would have shot him myself.

We brought Ink to the police department and interviewed him. Although he admitted he had shot the guy, he said he did it because the guy was an asshole. He didn't do it for the benefit of the NLR. He also said he wasn't an NLR member. He just hung out with them when he got put in prison.

He also refused to cooperate against the NLR or any NLR members he knew. From the evidence we gathered in the Ink investigation, the AUSA did not have any Federal charges that we could use against the NLR.

However, the Ink case was the first one that we worked together. It brought us together as a unit. It also became clear to everyone that I would provide direction and leadership to the task force. After the Ink case was over, the NLR Task Force let me take the reins. They followed my investigative plan, including the RICO charges against the NLR leadership.

THREE STOOGES

I mentioned Ricky Hahn before, I don't know if I mentioned it, but he was batshit crazy. There were many examples of Ricky Hahn's insanity. As I lived through this one, this is one that sticks in my mind.

The NLR Task Force had an NLR associate who was living in an apartment in Rancho Cucamonga who was on parole. Informant information came in that this person was an up and comer and was desperate to become a full-fledged NLR member. The informant also said the NLR associate was using methamphetamine and may also be selling it from his apartment.

I thought this NLR associate might be a good potential informant, so we decided to conduct a parole search on his apartment. Glenn Willett pulled his records, and it appeared that he lived in the apartment with his girlfriend.

We had seven NLR Task Force members, including myself, available for the raid. Glenn also called Ricky Hahn, as he was a San Bernardino County Sheriff's deputy, who worked in Rancho Cucamonga. Ricky was available so we headed over to the apartment and hooked up with him. He had worked with us in the past; he was a good guy. I loved working with Ricky.

The apartment was on the second floor. It was the first apartment on the second landing off the stairwell. There was a balcony with a sliding glass door. The balcony of the target apartment was facing the parking lot.

The plan was very simple. We would knock on the door with three guys. We would announce who we were and demand to be allowed to search the apartment. The rest of the team would set up around any escape routes in case the guy bolted on us. Once we secured the apartment, Glenn and I were going to interview the guy and assess his value as an informant, a piece of cake.

We knocked on the door and didn't get a response. A couple of guys from the team located the apartment manager. The manager told us our guy and his girlfriend were at work and not usually home during the day.

Since we had probable cause to conduct a parole search, Glenn convinced the apartment manager to open the subject's door with a pass key.

We did a quick safety check and verified the apartment was empty. We began a room-by-room parole search. We were looking for evidence of a crime and intelligence information relating to the NLR.

We found some pipes and drug paraphernalia related to methamphetamine usage. When we found him, Glenn planned on arresting the NLR associate for parole violation.

We had team members watching the front door of the apartment and parking lot for the subject. If he came, we didn't want to be surprised.

Suddenly the telephone in the apartment started ringing. At first, we were surprised because we hadn't expected it.

We let out some nervous laughter. Then Ricky picked up the telephone receiver. "Hello?" Ricky said. "Who is this? You called me, I didn't call you." Ricky said when questioned to his identity. "Oh, this is your place. Well I have been here rolling around in your bed."

The NLR associate was yelling so loud that all of us in the room could hear him. It was obvious that the guy was pissed off. Ricky kept pushing his buttons. "I saw the pictures of your girl. She is pretty hot. When does she get home from work?" There was more screaming from the telephone.

Ricky then said. "Hey, if you aren't going to talk nice to me I just going to take a shower and brush my teeth and leave. Is your tooth brush the red or purple one?"

The screaming got louder. Ricky held up the telephone receiver up and we could hear a string of obscenities from the NLR associate. Ricky laughed loudly into the telephone and hung up.

Seconds later, the telephone rang again. Ricky answered it on the third ring. "Yes?" Ricky held the receiver, so Glenn and I could hear what the NLR associate was saying. He said in a calm but threatening voice. "Dude, I am going to make you sorry that you were ever born. I am NLR and I am bringing some of my guys over there to deal with you." Ricky said. "Come ahead, I will be here." Then Ricky hung up.

We quickly briefed the guys in the parking lot and set up waiting for the NLR to show up.

We knew there were several NLR-associated guys coming to the apartment looking for at least a fight, but some of them may be armed. All of us on the raid had our body armor on and we were well armed with pistols and three shotguns and an MP5 10 mm submachine gun. We were ready for anything by the time they showed up.

There was no mistaking them when they got there. A red pickup came flying into the parking lot; there were two white guys in the bed of the pickup. They looked like NLR skinheads; they had bald heads, goatees, and were tattooed to the max. As an added flavor, they were both holding ax handles. When the truck pulled to a stop, the two NLR thugs jumped out of the truck bed obviously ready for action.

They paused at the back of the pickup waiting for the driver, and from the pictures that Glenn had shown us, I could see it was our NLR associate. The three of them stopped for a minute and then turned to the apartment.

The eight of us moved as one. We closed on them quickly and proned them out. The looks on their faces changed from purposeful determination to utter surprise and shock; it was comical. We handcuffed them and searched for weapons.

The NLR associate had an illegal switchblade. The other two goons had the ax handles, but that was all. The ax handles were decorated with swastikas, white supremacist signs, and NLR lettering.

We separated them to interview them. The NLR associate was hard core and wouldn't cooperate. The drug stuff and knife would get him six months in prison for parole violation, but he wouldn't roll. The other two guys were charged locally with brandishing a weapon for the ax handles. They really didn't know anything of use to the task force, and their records were petty crimes.

We put them together on the curb while waiting for transport by deputies to jail for booking. While we were waiting, we started asking them which one of them was Moe, Larry, and Curly, as they were the "Three Stooges" of the NLR. They didn't see the situation as funny as we did.

One other tradition that started at this arrest and carried through the rest of the NLR case: Ricky had a partner named Brad, who would show up occasionally to assist us on arrests. Brad was a Minnesota Vikings fan and being from Wisconsin, I was a diehard Green Bay Packers fan.

Since the teams are bitter rivals we started playing with the NLR suspects, as we were waiting for transport to the jail. Brad and I would tell the suspects that we had one final question for them, and if they answered right we would set them free.

The question was "Who is a better football team the Vikings or the Packers?" If they answered Packers, I would say, "Good job, let's get those cuffs off." Then Brad would say, "Nope, that's wrong, it is the Vikings, you are going to jail." Of course, if they answered Vikings, the roles would be reversed.

Needless to say, some of the suspects would find these antics irritating and launch into a tirade of obscenities. Others laughed with us and some were serious football fans who would argue that their favorite football teams were better than both the Vikings and Packers. It relieved tension and was fun.

FENCE

Being with the FBI in the late 1990s, we had some of the best equipment known to law enforcement. I had the best weapons and tactical equipment that I ever had since my law enforcement career started in 1983. I carried a 10 mm MP5 submachine gun, a Glock .40 cal, .357 Magnum Smith and Wesson revolver, two sets of steel handcuffs, a flashlight, pepper spray, and ASP baton. I wore level III body armor; it was blue with yellow FBI letters on the front and back.

The vest was capable of stopping a .44 Magnum revolver round and served as a carry platform for the aforementioned equipment. It was slightly larger and somewhat bulky as compared to vests that I had been issued in the past.

The only vest that I had that was bulkier was the SWAT ceramic body armor, which weighed about 50 pounds, but was capable of stopping a 7.62 mm rifle round. That damn thing killed your back after wearing it for a couple of hours.

The FBI also supplied equipment to task force members through the Safe Streets and Gang Task Force Unit at FBIHQ.

Usually, I was happy with the equipment. It functioned well, and I was confident that it would pull me through any intense situation. One night this same equipment almost did me in.

That night we found an NLR fugitive who we had been looking for several weeks in an apartment complex. It was not my case, and I was assigned to the back of the apartment complex to ensure the subject didn't escape on foot while the arrest team entered the apartment. I was with a uniformed officer from the local police department. We had been hitting residences that were related to the fugitive and his places to hide were getting scarce.

The plan was simple. The arrest team would go to the apartment, make contact, and ask for permission to search for the fugitive.

The resident was a relative of the fugitive, and we didn't have a search warrant, so the arrest team would have to finesse any search inside the apartment with the residents. The arrest team radioed that they were contacting the residents.

It seemed like things were going according to plan. They got inside the apartment and started searching. After about a half an hour, the arrest team came across the radio and said the fugitive wasn't in the apartment. The local officer got a call and asked if he could go, I figured we were finished at the apartment, so I told him to respond to his other call.

As I was waiting for the arrest team to clear, I noticed headlights coming into the parking lot. It was around midnight, so the vehicle traffic had been light. The car parked in an unlighted area of the parking lot. The driver was a male in a white tee shirt.

As I watched the driver walk across the parking lot, he passed no more than 20 feet from me. I recognized him as the fugitive. At the same time, the radio squawked as the arrest team was clearing the apartment. The fugitive focusing in on the sound of the radio saw me in the darkness.

He started running away from me, back through the parking lot. I tried the radio but someone was yapping as people often do after an operation. That was friggin irritating. I gotta admit I was pissed off. I started running after the fugitive on my own. I finally got the arrest team on the radio. They quickly joined me in the foot pursuit.

I saw the fugitive run up to an extremely high black metal fence. It was about 12 feet high and was topped with straight pointed spikes. The fence was at the end of the apartment parking lot and bordered a concrete spillway. The fugitive must have been familiar with the area because he never even slowed down when he hit the fence line.

He was up and over in a flash. He jumped down to the base of the fence and lowered himself into the spillway, another 10 feet. I called out where we were and continued the foot pursuit.

I hit the fence running and used the supports in the fence as foot and hand holds to scale the 12-foot fence. I did pretty well too, until I got to the

177

top. I looked down at the 20-foot drop to the bottom of the concrete spill-way and got nervous and cautious. I tried to lower myself down slowly, feet first.

Unfortunately, two of the pointed spear tops slipped between my back and the level III body armor. My grip on the top of the fence slipped and the two spear points slipped about two feet in between my body armor and my back. I was stuck on the fence about 20 feet up in the air, helpless as a kitten up a tree.

I saw the fugitive's white tee shirt disappear down the spillway. I called his last position out on the radio. The arrest team was trying to set up a perimeter and asked for my position, so I had to reluctantly give it to them.

Luckily, the local cops sent some units up the spillway and caught the fugitive not far from where I last sighted him. A couple of the NLR Task Force guys found some ladders and helped me off the fence.

For weeks, I had to endure the barbs and jokes of the task force guys about "hanging around" and being the "eye in the sky." It was very embarrassing.

I am glad I didn't fall in the spillway; embarrassed is one thing, and getting hurt was another.

These are just a few of the experiences that I had while working the NLR case. I have many more; a major investigation is like life itself, full of ups and downs. For every two steps you take forward, you are bound to take one back.

The experience was rewarding and educational. I learned and honed my skills as a leader and investigator.

The NLR investigation was a high point in my career as a street agent. It led me to other endeavors such as taking a promotion to FBIHQ to work in the SSGU.

This move also put me in Washington DC on September 11, 2001. Watching the black smoke from the Pentagon from FBIHQ, and waiting for orders to react was another life-altering experience.

Then, I had the opportunity to apply the Criminal Enterprise Investigation (CEI) techniques in the counterterrorism arena in Iraq in 2007. The CEI techniques have allowed me to tackle the most challenging organizations and effectively disrupt and dismantle their operations.

I hope this book will assist law enforcement and security profession-als understand and apply the CEI concept.

APPENDIX
Statutes

18 USC 924: Penalties

From Title 18—CRIMES AND CRIMINAL PROCEDURE
PART I—CRIMES
CHAPTER 44—FIREARMS
§924. Penalties

(a) (1) Except as otherwise provided in this subsection, subsection (b), (c), (f), or (p) of this section, or in section 929, whoever—

(A) Knowingly makes any false statement or representation with respect to the information required by this chapter to be kept in the records of a person licensed under this chapter or in applying for any license or exemption or relief from disability under the provisions of this chapter;

(B) Knowingly violates subsection (a)(4), (f), (k), or (q) of section 922;

(C) Knowingly imports or brings into the United States or any possession thereof any firearm or ammunition in violation of section 922(l); or

(D) Willfully violates any other provision of this chapter, shall be fined under this title, imprisoned not more than five years, or both

(2) Whoever knowingly violates subsection (a)(6), (d), (g), (h), (i), (j), or (o) of section 922 shall be fined as provided in this title, imprisoned not more than 10 years, or both

(3) Any licensed dealer, licensed importer, licensed manufacturer, or licensed collector who knowingly—

(A) Makes any false statement or representation with respect to the information required by the provisions of this chapter to be kept in the records of a person licensed under this chapter, or

(B) Violates subsection (m) of section 922, shall be fined under this title, imprisoned not more than one year, or both

(4) Whoever violates section 922(q) shall be fined under this title, imprisoned for not more than 5 years, or both. Notwithstanding any other provision of law, the term of imprisonment imposed under this paragraph shall not run concurrently with any other term of imprisonment imposed under any other provision of law. Except for the authorization of a term of imprisonment of not more than 5 years made in this paragraph, for the purpose of any other law a violation of section 922(q) shall be deemed to be a misdemeanor.

(5) Whoever knowingly violates subsection (s) or (t) of section 922 shall be fined under this title, imprisoned for not more than 1 year, or both

(6) (A)(i) A Juvenile who violates section 922(x) shall be fined under this title, imprisoned not more than 1 year, or both, except that a juvenile described in clause (ii) shall be sentenced to probation on appropriate conditions and shall not be incarcerated unless the juvenile fails to comply with a condition of probation.

(ii) A juvenile is described in this clause if—

(I) the offense of which the juvenile is charged is possession of a handgun or ammunition in violation of section 922(x) (2); and

(II) the juvenile has not been convicted in any court of an offense (including an offense under section 922(x) or a similar State law, but not including any other offense consisting of conduct that if engaged in by an adult would not constitute an offense) or adjudicated as a juvenile delinquent for conduct that if engaged in by an adult would constitute an offense.

(B) A Person other than a juvenile who knowingly violates section 922(x)-

(i) shall be fined under this title, imprisoned not more than 1 year, or both; and

(ii) if the person sold, delivered, or otherwise transferred a handgun or ammunition to a juvenile knowing or having reasonable cause to know that the juvenile intended to carry or otherwise possess or discharge or otherwise use the handgun or ammunition in the commission of a crime of violence, shall be fined under this title, imprisoned not more than 10 years, or both.

(7) Whoever knowingly violates section 931 shall be fined under this title, imprisoned not more than 3 years, or both

(b) Whoever, with intent to commit therewith an offense punishable by imprisonment for a term exceeding one year, or with knowledge or reasonable cause to believe that an offense punishable by imprisonment for a term exceeding one year is to be committed therewith, ships, transports, or receives a firearm or any ammunition in interstate or foreign commerce shall be fined under this title, or imprisoned not more than ten years, or both

(c) (1) (A) Except to the extent that a greater minimum sentence is otherwise provided by this subsection or by any other provision of law, any person who, during and in relation to any crime of violence or drug trafficking crime (including a crime of violence or drug trafficking crime that provides for an enhanced punishment if committed by the use of a deadly or dangerous weapon or device) for which the person may be prosecuted in a court of the United States, uses or carries a firearm, or who, in furtherance of any such crime, possesses a firearm, shall, in addition to the punishment provided for such crime of violence or drug trafficking crime-

(i) be sentenced to a term of imprisonment of not less than 5 years;

(ii) if the firearm is brandished, be sentenced to a term of imprisonment of not less than 7 years; and

(iii) if the firearm is discharged, be sentenced to a term of imprisonment of not less than 10 years.

(B) If the firearm possessed by a person convicted of a violation of this subsection-

(i) is a short-barreled rifle, short-barreled shotgun, or semiautomatic assault weapon, the person shall be sentenced to a term of imprisonment of not less than 10 years; or

(ii) is a machinegun or a destructive device, or is equipped with a firearm silencer or firearm muffler, the person shall be sentenced to a term of imprisonment of not less than 30 years.

(C) In the case of a second or subsequent conviction under this subsection, the person shall—

(i) be sentenced to a term of imprisonment of not less than 25 years; and

       (ii) if the firearm involved is a machinegun or a destructive device, or is equipped with a firearm silencer or firearm muffler, be sentenced to imprisonment for life.

(D) Notwithstanding any other provision of law—

       (i) a court shall not place on probation any person convicted of a violation of this subsection; and

      (ii) no term of imprisonment imposed on a person under this subsection shall run concurrently with any other term of imprisonment imposed on the person, including any term of imprisonment imposed for the crime of violence or drug trafficking crime during which the firearm was used, carried, or possessed.

(2) For purposes of this subsection, the term "drug trafficking crime" means any felony punishable under the Controlled Substances Act (21 U.S.C. 801 et seq.), the Controlled Substances Import and Export Act (21 U.S.C. 951 et seq.), or chapter 705 of title 46

(3) For purposes of this subsection the term "crime of violence" means an offense that is a felony and—

(A) Has as an element the use, attempted use, or threatened use of physical force against the person or property of another, or

(B) That by its nature, involves a substantial risk that physical force against the person or property of another may be used in the course of committing the offense

(4) For purposes of this subsection, the term "brandish" means, with respect to a firearm, to display all or part of the firearm, or otherwise make the presence of the firearm known to another person, in order to intimidate that person, regardless of whether the firearm is directly visible to that person

(5) Except to the extent that a greater minimum sentence is otherwise provided under this subsection, or by any other provision of law, any person who, during and in relation to any crime of violence or drug trafficking crime (including a crime of violence or drug trafficking crime that provides for an enhanced punishment if committed by the use of a deadly or dangerous weapon or device) for which the person may be prosecuted in a court of the United States, uses or carries armor piercing ammunition, or who, in furtherance of any such crime, possesses armor piercing ammunition, shall, in addition to the punishment provided for such crime of violence or drug trafficking crime or conviction under this section—

(A) Be sentenced to a term of imprisonment of not less than 15 years; and

(B) If death results from the use of such ammunition—

(i) if the killing is murder (as defined in section 1111), be punished by death or sentenced to a term of imprisonment for any term of years or for life; and

(ii) if the killing is manslaughter (as defined in section 1112), be punished as provided in section 1112.

(d) (1) Any firearm or ammunition involved in or used in any knowing violation of subsection (a)(4), (a)(6), (f), (g), (h), (i), (j), or (k) of section 922, or knowing importation or bringing into the United States or any possession thereof any firearm or ammunition in violation of section 922(l), or knowing violation of section 924, or willful violation of any other provision of this chapter or any rule or regulation promulgated thereunder, or any violation of any other criminal law of the United States, or any firearm or ammunition intended to be used in any offense referred to in paragraph (3) of this subsection, where such intent is demonstrated by clear and convincing evidence, shall be subject to seizure and forfeiture, and all provisions of the Internal Revenue Code of 1986 relating to the seizure, forfeiture, and disposition of firearms, as defined in section 5845(a) of that Code, shall, so far as applicable, extend to seizures and forfeitures under the provisions of this chapter: Provided, That upon acquittal of the owner or possessor, or dismissal of the charges against him other than upon motion of the Government prior to trial, or lapse of or court termination of the restraining order to which he is subject, the seized or relinquished firearms or ammunition shall be returned forthwith to the owner or possessor or to a person delegated by the owner or possessor unless the return of the firearms or ammunition would place the owner or possessor or his delegate in violation of law. Any action or proceeding for the forfeiture of firearms or ammunition shall be commenced within one hundred and twenty days of such seizure

(2) (A) In any action or proceeding for the return of firearms or ammunition seized under the provisions of this chapter, the court shall allow the prevailing party, other than the United States, a reasonable attorney's fee, and the United States shall be liable therefor.

(B) In any other action or proceeding under the provisions of this chapter, the court, when it finds that such action was without foundation, or was initiated vexatiously, frivolously, or in bad faith, shall allow the prevailing party, other than the United States, a reasonable attorney's fee, and the United States shall be liable therefor.

(C) Only those firearms or quantities of ammunition particularly named and individually identified as involved in or used in any violation of the provisions of this chapter or any rule or regulation issued thereunder, or any other criminal law of the United States or as intended to be used in any offense referred to in paragraph (3) of this subsection, where such intent is demonstrated by clear and convincing evidence, shall be subject to seizure, forfeiture, and disposition.

(D) The United States shall be liable for attorneys' fees under this paragraph only to the extent provided in advance by appropriation Acts.

(3) (1) and (2)(C) of this subsection are—

(A) Any crime of violence, as that term is defined in section 924(c)(3) of this title;

(B) Any offense punishable under the Controlled Substances Act (21 U.S.C. 801 et seq.) or the Controlled Substances Import and Export Act (21 U.S.C. 951 et seq.);

(C) Any offense described in section 922(a)(1), 922(a)(3), 922(a)(5), or 922(b)(3) of this title, where the firearm or ammunition intended to be used in any such offense is involved in a pattern of activities which includes a violation of any offense described in section 922(a)(1), 922(a)(3), 922(a)(5), or 922(b)(3) of this title;

(D) Any offense described in section 922(d) of this title where the firearm or ammunition is intended to be used in such offense by the transferor of such firearm or ammunition;

(E) Any offense described in section 922(i), 922(j), 922(l), 922(n), or 924(b) of this title; and

(F) Any offense which may be prosecuted in a court of the United States which involves the exportation of firearms or ammunition

(e) (1) In the case of a person who violates section 922(g) of this title and has three previous convictions by any court referred to in section 922(g)(1) of this title for a violent felony or a serious drug

184

offense, or both, committed on occasions different from one another, such person shall be fined under this title and imprisoned not less than fifteen years, and, notwithstanding any other provision of law, the court shall not suspend the sentence of, or grant a probationary sentence to, such person with respect to the conviction under section 922(g)

(2) As used in this subsection—

    (A) The term "serious drug offense" means—

        (i) an offense under the Controlled Substances Act (21 U.S.C. 801 et seq.), the Controlled Substances Import and Export Act (21 U.S.C. 951 et seq.), or chapter 705 of title 46 for which a maximum term of imprisonment of ten years or more is prescribed by law; or

        (ii) an offense under State law, involving manufacturing, distributing, or possessing with intent to manufacture or distribute, a controlled substance (as defined in section 102 of the Controlled Substances Act (21 U.S.C. 802)), for which a maximum term of imprisonment of ten years or more is prescribed by law;

    (B) The term "violent felony" means any crime punishable by imprisonment for a term exceeding one year, or any act of juvenile delinquency involving the use or carrying of a firearm, knife, or destructive device that would be punishable by imprisonment for such term if committed by an adult, that-

        (i) has as an element the use, attempted use, or threatened use of physical force against the person of another; or

        (ii) is burglary, arson, or extortion, involves use of explosives, or otherwise involves conduct that presents a serious potential risk of physical injury to another; and

    (C) The term "conviction" includes a finding that a person has committed an act of juvenile delinquency involving a violent felony

(f) In the case of a person who knowingly violates section 922(p), such person shall be fined under this title, or imprisoned not more than 5 years, or both

(g) Whoever, with the intent to engage in conduct which—

    (1) Constitutes an offense listed in section 1961(1),

    (2) Is punishable under the Controlled Substances Act (21 U.S.C. 801 et seq.), the Controlled Substances Import and Export Act (21 U.S.C. 951 et seq.), or chapter 705 of title 46,

(3) Violates any State law relating to any controlled substance (as defined in section 102(6) of the Controlled Substances Act (21 U.S.C. 802(6))), or

(4) Constitutes a crime of violence (as defined in subsection (c)(3)), travels from any State or foreign country into any other State and acquires, transfers, or attempts to acquire or transfer, a firearm in such other State in furtherance of such purpose, shall be imprisoned not more than 10 years, fined in accordance with this title, or both

(h) Whoever knowingly transfers a firearm, knowing that such firearm will be used to commit a crime of violence (as defined in subsection (c)(3)) or drug trafficking crime (as defined in subsection (c)(2)) shall be imprisoned not more than 10 years, fined in accordance with this title, or both

(i) (1) A Person who knowingly violates section 922(u) shall be fined under this title, imprisoned not more than 10 years, or both

(2) Nothing contained in this subsection shall be construed as indicating an intent on the part of Congress to occupy the field in which provisions of this subsection operate to the exclusion of State laws on the same subject matter, nor shall any provision of this subsection be construed as invalidating any provision of State law unless such provision is inconsistent with any of the purposes of this subsection

(j) A Person who, in the course of a violation of subsection (c), causes the death of a person through the use of a firearm, shall—

(1) If the killing is a murder (as defined in section 1111), be punished by death or by imprisonment for any term of years or for life; and

(2) If the killing is manslaughter (as defined in section 1112), be punished as provided in that section

(k) A Person who, with intent to engage in or to promote conduct that—

(1) Is punishable under the Controlled Substances Act (21 U.S.C. 801 et seq.), the Controlled Substances Import and Export Act (21 U.S.C. 951 et seq.), or chapter 705 of title 46;

(2) Violates any law of a State relating to any controlled substance (as defined in section 102 of the Controlled Substances Act, 21 U.S.C. 802); or

(3) Constitutes a crime of violence (as defined in subsection (c) (3)), smuggles or knowingly brings into the United States a

firearm, or attempts to do so, shall be imprisoned not more than 10 years, fined under this title, or both

(l) A Person who steals any firearm which is moving as, or is a part of, or which has moved in, interstate or foreign commerce shall be imprisoned for not more than 10 years, fined under this title, or both

(m) A Person who steals any firearm from a licensed importer, licensed manufacturer, licensed dealer, or licensed collector shall be fined under this title, imprisoned not more than 10 years, or both

(n)A Person who, with the intent to engage in conduct that constitutes a violation of section 922(a)(1)(A), travels from any State or foreign country into any other State and acquires, or attempts to acquire, a firearm in such other State in furtherance of such purpose shall be imprisoned for not more than 10 years

(o)A Person who conspires to commit an offense under subsection (c) shall be imprisoned for not more than 20 years, fined under this title, or both; and if the firearm is a machinegun or destructive device, or is equipped with a firearm silencer or muffler, shall be imprisoned for any term of years or life

(p)Penalties relating to secure gun storage or safety device—

(1) In general—

   (A) Suspension or revocation of license; civil penalties—With respect to each violation of section 922(z)(1) by a licensed manufacturer, licensed importer, or licensed dealer, the Secretary may, after notice and opportunity for hearing—

      (i)   suspend for not more than 6 months, or revoke, the license issued to the licensee under this chapter that was used to conduct the firearms transfer; or

      (ii) subject the licensee to a civil penalty in an amount equal to not more than $2,500.

   (B) Review—An action of the Secretary under this paragraph may be reviewed only as provided under section 923(f)

RICO USC Title 18 Section §1961.

Definitions
As used in this chapter—

(1) "Racketeering activity" means (A) any act or threat involving murder, kidnapping, gambling, arson, robbery, bribery, extortion, dealing in obscene matter, or dealing in a controlled substance or listed chemical (as defined in section 102 of the Controlled

Substances Act), which is chargeable under State law and punishable by imprisonment for more than one year; (B) any act which is indictable under any of the following provisions of title 18, United States Code: Section 201 (relating to bribery), section 224 (relating to sports bribery), sections 471, 472, and 473 (relating to counterfeiting), section 659 (relating to theft from interstate shipment) if the act indictable under section 659 is felonious, section 664 (relating to embezzlement from pension and welfare funds), sections 891–894 (relating to extortionate credit transactions), section 1028 (relating to fraud and related activity in connection with identification documents), section 1029 (relating to fraud and related activity in connection with access devices), section 1084 (relating to the transmission of gambling information), section 1341 (relating to mail fraud), section 1343 (relating to wire fraud), section 1344 (relating to financial institution fraud), section 1351 (relating to fraud in foreign labor contracting), section 1425 (relating to the procurement of citizenship or nationalization unlawfully), section 1426 (relating to the reproduction of naturalization or citizenship papers), section 1427 (relating to the sale of naturalization or citizenship papers), sections 1461–1465 (relating to obscene matter), section 1503 (relating to obstruction of justice), section 1510 (relating to obstruction of criminal investigations), section 1511 (relating to the obstruction of State or local law enforcement), section 1512 (relating to tampering with a witness, victim, or an informant), section 1513 (relating to retaliating against a witness, victim, or an informant), section 1542 (relating to false statement in application and use of passport), section 1543 (relating to forgery or false use of passport), section 1544 (relating to misuse of passport), section 1546 (relating to fraud and misuse of visas, permits, and other documents), sections 1581–1592 (relating to peonage, slavery, and trafficking in persons)., 1 section 1951 (relating to interference with commerce, robbery, or extortion), section 1952 (relating to racketeering), section 1953 (relating to interstate transportation of wagering paraphernalia), section 1954 (relating to unlawful welfare fund payments), section 1955 (relating to the prohibition of illegal gambling businesses), section 1956 (relating to the laundering of monetary instruments), section 1957 (relating to engaging in monetary transactions in property derived from specified unlawful activity), section 1958 (relating to use of interstate commerce facilities in the commission of murder-for-hire), section 1960 (relating to illegal money transmitters), sections 2251, 2251A, 2252, and 2260 (relating to sexual exploitation of children), sections 2312 and 2313 (relating to interstate transportation of stolen motor vehicles), sections 2314 and 2315 (relating to interstate transportation of stolen property), section 2318 (relating to trafficking in counterfeit labels for phonorecords, computer programs or computer program documentation or packaging and copies of motion pictures or other audiovisual works), section 2319 (relating to criminal infringement of a copyright), section 2319A (relating to unauthorized fixation of and trafficking in sound recordings and music videos of live musical performances), section 2320 (relating to trafficking in goods or services bearing counterfeit marks), section 2321 (relating to trafficking in certain motor vehicles or motor vehicle parts), sections 2341–2346 (relating to trafficking in contraband cigarettes), sections 2421–24 (relating to white slave traffic), sections 175–178 (relating to biological weapons), sections 229–229F (relating to chemical weapons), section 831 (relating to nuclear materials), (C) any act which is indictable under title 29, United States Code, section 186 (dealing with restrictions on payments and loans to labor organizations) or section 501(c) (relating to embezzlement from union funds), (D) any offense involving fraud connected with a case under title 11 (except a case under section 157 of this title), fraud in the sale of securities, or the felonious manufacture, importation, receiving, concealment, buying, selling, or otherwise dealing in a controlled substance or listed chemical (as defined in section 102 of the Controlled Substances Act), punishable under any law of the United States, (E) any act which is indictable under the Currency and Foreign Transactions Reporting Act, (F) any act which is indictable under the Immigration and Nationality Act, section 274 (relating to bringing in and harboring certain aliens), section 277 (relating to aiding or assisting certain aliens to enter the United States), or section 278 (relating to importation of alien for immoral purpose) if the act indictable under such section of such Act was committed for the purpose of financial gain, or (G) any act that is indictable under any provision listed in section 2332b(g)(5)(B);

(2) "State" means any State of the United States, the District of Columbia, the Commonwealth of Puerto Rico, any territory or possession of the United States, any political subdivision, or any department, agency, or instrumentality thereof;

(3) "Person" includes any individual or entity capable of holding a legal or beneficial interest in property;

(4) "Enterprise" includes any individual, partnership, corporation, association, or other legal entity, and any union or group of individuals associated in fact although not a legal entity;

(5) "Pattern of racketeering activity" requires at least two acts of racketeering activity, one of which occurred after the effective date of this chapter and the last of which occurred within ten years (excluding any period of imprisonment) after the commission of a prior act of racketeering activity;

(6) "Unlawful debt" means a debt (A) incurred or contracted in gambling activity which was in violation of the law of the United States, a State or political subdivision thereof, or which is unenforceable under State or Federal law in whole or in part as to principal or interest because of the laws relating to usury, and (B) which was incurred in connection with the business of gambling in violation of the law of the United States, a State or political subdivision thereof, or the business of lending money or a thing of value at a rate usurious under State or Federal law, where the usurious rate is at least twice the enforceable rate;

(7) "Racketeering investigator" means any attorney or investigator so designated by the Attorney General and charged with the duty of enforcing or carrying into effect this chapter;

(8) "Racketeering investigation" means any inquiry conducted by any racketeering investigator for the purpose of ascertaining whether any person has been involved in any violation of this chapter or of any final order, judgment, or decree of any court of the United States, duly entered in any case or proceeding arising under this chapter;

(9) "Documentary material" includes any book, paper, document, record, recording, or other material; and

(10) "Attorney General" includes the Attorney General of the United States, the Deputy Attorney General of the United States, the Associate Attorney General of the United States, any Assistant Attorney General of the United States, or any employee of the Department of Justice or any employee of any department or agency of the United States so designated by the Attorney General to carry out the powers conferred on the Attorney General by this chapter. Any department or agency so designated may use in investigations authorized by this chapter

either the investigative provisions of this chapter or the investigative power of such department or agency otherwise conferred by law

18 USC 1791: Providing or possessing contraband in prison

From Title 18—CRIMES AND CRIMINAL PROCEDURE
PART I—CRIMES
CHAPTER 87—PRISONS
§1791. Providing or possessing contraband in prison

(a) Offense—Whoever—
  (1) In violation of a statute or a rule or order issued under a statute, provides to an inmate of a prison a prohibited object, or attempts to do so; or
  (2) Being an inmate of a prison, makes, possesses, or obtains, or attempts to make or obtain, a prohibited object; shall be punished as provided in subsection (b) of this section

(b) Punishment—The punishment for an offense under this section is a fine under this title or—
  (1) Imprisonment for not more than 20 years, or both, if the object is specified in subsection (d)(1)(C) of this section;
  (2) Imprisonment for not more than 10 years, or both, if the object is specified in subsection (d)(1)(A) of this section;
  (3) Imprisonment for not more than 5 years, or both, if the object is specified in subsection (d)(1)(B) of this section;
  (4) Imprisonment for not more than one year, or both, if the object is specified in subsection (d)(1)(D), (d)(1)(E), or (d)(1)(F) of this section; and
  (5) Imprisonment for not more than 6 months, or both, if the object is specified in subsection (d)(1)(G) of this section.

(c) Consecutive Punishment Required in Certain Cases—Any punishment imposed under subsection (b) for a violation of this section involving a controlled substance shall be consecutive to any other sentence imposed by any court for an offense involving such a controlled substance. Any punishment imposed under subsection (b) for a violation of this section by an inmate of a prison shall be consecutive to the sentence being served by such inmate at the time the inmate commits such violation

(d) Definitions—As used in this section—
  (1) The term "prohibited object" means—

(A) a firearm or destructive device or a controlled substance in schedule I or II, other than marijuana or a controlled substance referred to in subparagraph (C) of this subsection;

(B) marijuana or a controlled substance in schedule III, other than a controlled substance referred to in subparagraph (C) of this subsection, ammunition, a weapon (other than a firearm or destructive device), or an object that is designed or intended to be used as a weapon or to facilitate escape from a prison;

(C) a narcotic drug, methamphetamine, its salts, isomers, and salts of its isomers, lysergic acid diethylamide, or phencyclidine;

(D) a controlled substance (other than a controlled substance referred to in subparagraph (A), (B), or (C) of this subsection) or an alcoholic beverage;

(E) any United States or foreign currency;

(F) a phone or other device used by a user of commercial mobile service (as defined in section 332(d) of the Communications Act of 1934 (47 U.S.C. 332(d))) in connection with such service; and

(G) any other object that threatens the order, discipline, or security of a prison, or the life, health, or safety of an individual;

(2) The terms "ammunition," "firearm," and "destructive device" have, respectively, the meanings given those terms in section 921 of this title;

(3) The terms "controlled substance" and "narcotic drug" have, respectively, the meanings given those terms in section 102 of the Controlled Substances Act (21 U.S.C. 802); and

(4) The term "prison" means a Federal correctional, detention, or penal facility or any prison, institution, or facility in which persons are held in custody by direction of or pursuant to a contract or agreement with the Attorney General.

18 USC 1956: Laundering of monetary instruments

Text contains those laws in effect on September 1, 2015
From Title 18—CRIMES AND CRIMINAL PROCEDURE
PART I—CRIMES
CHAPTER 95—RACKETEERING
§1956. Laundering of monetary instruments

(a) (1) Whoever, knowing that the property involved in a financial transaction represents the proceeds of some form of unlawful activity, conducts or attempts to conduct such a financial transaction which in fact involves the proceeds of specified unlawful activity—

    (A) (i) With the intent to promote the carrying on of specified unlawful activity; or

        (ii) With intent to engage in conduct constituting a violation of section 7201 or 7206 of the Internal Revenue Code of 1986; or

    (B) Knowing that the transaction is designed in whole or in part—

        (i) to conceal or disguise the nature, the location, the source, the ownership, or the control of the proceeds of specified unlawful activity; or

        (ii) to avoid a transaction reporting requirement under State or Federal law, shall be sentenced to a fine of not more than $500,000 or twice the value of the property involved in the transaction, whichever is greater, or imprisonment for not more than twenty years, or both. For purposes of this paragraph, a financial transaction shall be considered to be one involving the proceeds of specified unlawful activity if it is part of a set of parallel or dependent transactions, any one of which involves the proceeds of specified unlawful activity, and all of which are part of a single plan or arrangement.

(2) Whoever transports, transmits, or transfers, or attempts to transport, transmit, or transfer a monetary instrument or funds from a place in the United States to or through a place outside the United States or to a place in the United States from or through a place outside the United States—

    (A) With the intent to promote the carrying on of specified unlawful activity; or

    (B) Knowing that the monetary instrument or funds involved in the transportation, transmission, or transfer represent the proceeds of some form of unlawful activity and knowing that such transportation, transmission, or transfer is designed in whole or in part—

        (i) to conceal or disguise the nature, the location, the source, the ownership, or the control of the proceeds of specified unlawful activity; or

       (ii) to avoid a transaction reporting requirement under State or Federal law, shall be sentenced to a fine of not more than $500,000 or twice the value of the monetary instrument or funds involved in the transportation, transmission, or transfer, whichever is greater, or imprisonment for not more than twenty years, or both. For the purpose of the offense described in subparagraph (B), the defendant's knowledge may be established by proof that a law enforcement officer represented the matter specified in subparagraph (B) as true, and the defendant's subsequent statements or actions indicate that the defendant believed such representations to be true.

(3) Whoever, with the intent—

   (A) To promote the carrying on of specified unlawful activity;

   (B) To conceal or disguise the nature, location, source, ownership, or control of property believed to be the proceeds of specified unlawful activity; or

   (C) To avoid a transaction reporting requirement under State or Federal law, conducts or attempts to conduct a financial transaction involving property represented to be the proceeds of specified unlawful activity, or property used to conduct or facilitate specified unlawful activity, shall be fined under this title or imprisoned for not more than 20 years, or both. For purposes of this paragraph and paragraph (2), the term "represented" means any representation made by a law enforcement officer or by another person at the direction of, or with the approval of, a Federal official authorized to investigate or prosecute violations of this section

(b) Penalties—

(1) In general—Whoever conducts or attempts to conduct a transaction described in subsection (a)(1) or (a)(3), or section 1957, or a transportation, transmission, or transfer described in subsection (a)(2), is liable to the United States for a civil penalty of not more than the greater of—

   (A) The value of the property, funds, or monetary instruments involved in the transaction; or

   (B) $10,000

(2) Jurisdiction over foreign persons—For purposes of adjudicating an action filed or enforcing a penalty ordered under this section, the district courts shall have jurisdiction over any foreign person,

including any financial institution authorized under the laws of a foreign country, against whom the action is brought, if service of process upon the foreign person is made under the Federal Rules of Civil Procedure or the laws of the country in which the foreign person is found, and—

(A) the foreign person commits an offense under subsection (a) involving a financial transaction that occurs in whole or in part in the United States;

(B) the foreign person converts, to his or her own use, property in which the United States has an ownership interest by virtue of the entry of an order of forfeiture by a court of the United States; or

(C) the foreign person is a financial institution that maintains a bank account at a financial institution in the United States.

(3) Court authority over assets—A court may issue a pretrial restraining order or take any other action necessary to ensure that any bank account or other property held by the defendant in the United States is available to satisfy a judgment under this section.

(4) Federal receiver—

(A) In general—A court may appoint a Federal Receiver, in accordance with subparagraph (B) of this paragraph, to collect, marshal, and take custody, control, and possession of all assets of the defendant, wherever located, to satisfy a civil judgment under this subsection, a forfeiture judgment under section 981 or 982, or a criminal sentence under section 1957 or subsection (a) of this section, including an order of restitution to any victim of a specified unlawful activity.

(B) Appointment and authority—A Federal Receiver described in subparagraph (A)—

(i) may be appointed upon application of a Federal prosecutor or a Federal or State regulator, by the court having jurisdiction over the defendant in the case;

(ii) shall be an officer of the court, and the powers of the Federal Receiver shall include the powers set out in section 754 of title 28, United States Code; and

(iii) shall have standing equivalent to that of a Federal prosecutor for the purpose of submitting requests to obtain information regarding the assets of the defendant-

(I) from the Financial Crimes Enforcement Network of the Department of the Treasury; or

(II) from a foreign country pursuant to a mutual legal assistance treaty, multilateral agreement, or other arrangement for international law enforcement assistance, provided that such requests are in accordance with the policies and procedures of the Attorney General.

(c) As used in this section—

(1) The term "knowing that the property involved in a financial transaction represents the proceeds of some form of unlawful activity" means that the person knew the property involved in the transaction represented proceeds from some form, though not necessarily which form, of activity that constitutes a felony under State, Federal, or foreign law, regardless of whether or not such activity is specified in paragraph (7);

(2) The term "conducts" includes initiating, concluding, or participating in initiating, or concluding a transaction;

(3) The term "transaction" includes a purchase, sale, loan, pledge, gift, transfer, delivery, or other disposition, and with respect to a financial institution includes a deposit, withdrawal, transfer between accounts, exchange of currency, loan, extension of credit, purchase or sale of any stock, bond, certificate of deposit, or other monetary instrument, use of a safe deposit box, or any other payment, transfer, or delivery by, through, or to a financial institution, by whatever means effected;

(4) The term "financial transaction" means (A) a transaction which in any way or degree affects interstate or foreign commerce (i) involving the movement of funds by wire or other means or (ii) involving one or more monetary instruments, or (iii) involving the transfer of title to any real property, vehicle, vessel, or aircraft, or (B) a transaction involving the use of a financial institution which is engaged in, or the activities of which affect, interstate or foreign commerce in any way or degree;

(5) The term "monetary instruments" means (i) coin or currency of the United States or of any other country, travelers' checks, personal checks, bank checks, and money orders, or (ii) investment securities or negotiable instruments, in bearer form or otherwise in such form that title thereto passes upon delivery;

(6) The term "financial institution" includes—

(A) any financial institution, as defined in section 5312(a)(2) of title 31, United States Code, or the regulations promulgated thereunder; and

(B) any foreign bank, as defined in section 1 of the International Banking Act of 1978 (12 U.S.C. 3101);

(7) The term "specified unlawful activity" means—

(A) any act or activity constituting an offense listed in section 1961(1) of this title except an act which is indictable under subchapter II of chapter 53 of title 31;

(B) with respect to a financial transaction occurring in whole or in part in the United States, an offense against a foreign nation involving—

    (i)   the manufacture, importation, sale, or distribution of a controlled substance (as such term is defined for the purposes of the Controlled Substances Act);

    (ii) murder, kidnapping, robbery, extortion, destruction of property by means of explosive or fire, or a crime of violence (as defined in section 16);

    (iii) fraud, or any scheme or attempt to defraud, by or against a foreign bank (as defined in paragraph 7 of section 1(b) of the International Banking Act of 1978)); 1

    (iv) bribery of a public official, or the misappropriation, theft, or embezzlement of public funds by or for the benefit of a public official;

    (v)   smuggling or export control violations involving—

        (I) an item controlled on the United States Munitions List established under section 38 of the Arms Export Control Act (22 U.S.C. 2778); or

        (II) an item controlled under regulations under the Export Administration Regulations (15 C.F.R. Parts 730–774);

    (vi) an offense with respect to which the United States would be obligated by a multilateral treaty, either to extradite the alleged offender or to submit the case for prosecution, if the offender were found within the territory of the United States; or

    (vii) trafficking in persons, selling or buying of children, sexual exploitation of children, or transporting, recruiting or harboring a person, including a child, for commercial sex acts;

(C) any act or acts constituting a continuing criminal enterprise, as that term is defined in section 408 of the Controlled Substances Act (21 U.S.C. 848);

(D) an offense under section 32 (relating to the destruction of aircraft), section 37 (relating to violence at international airports), section 115 (relating to influencing, impeding, or retaliating against a Federal official by threatening or injuring a family member), section 152 (relating to concealment of assets; false oaths and claims; bribery), section 175c (relating to the variola virus), section 215 (relating to commissions or gifts for procuring loans), section 351 (relating to congressional or Cabinet officer assassination), any of sections 500 through 503 (relating to certain counterfeiting offenses), section 513 (relating to securities of States and private entities), section 541 (relating to goods falsely classified), section 542 (relating to entry of goods by means of false statements), section 545 (relating to smuggling goods into the United States), section 549 (relating to removing goods from Customs custody), section 554 (relating to smuggling goods from the United States), section 555 (relating to border tunnels), section 641 (relating to public money, property, or records), section 656 (relating to theft, embezzlement, or misapplication by bank officer or employee), section 657 (relating to lending, credit, and insurance institutions), section 658 (relating to property mortgaged or pledged to farm credit agencies), section 666 (relating to theft or bribery concerning programs receiving Federal funds), section 793, 794, or 798 (relating to espionage), section 831 (relating to prohibited transactions involving nuclear materials), section 844(f) or (i) (relating to destruction by explosives or fire of Government property or property affecting interstate or foreign commerce), section 875 (relating to interstate communications), section 922(l) (relating to the unlawful importation of firearms), section 924(n) (relating to firearms trafficking), section 956 (relating to conspiracy to kill, kidnap, maim, or injure certain property in a foreign country), section 1005 (relating to fraudulent bank entries), 1006 2 (relating to fraudulent Federal credit institution entries), 1007 2 (relating to Federal Deposit Insurance transactions), 1014 2 (relating to fraudulent loan or credit applications), section 1030 (relating to computer fraud and abuse), 1032 2 (relating to concealment of assets from conservator, receiver, or liquidating agent of financial institution), section 1111 (relating to murder), section 1114 (relating to murder of United States law enforcement officials), section 1116 (relating to murder of foreign officials, official guests, or internationally protected persons), section 1201 (relating to kidnapping), section 1203 (relating to hostage taking), section 1361 (relating to willful injury of Government property), section 1363 (relating to destruction of property within the special maritime and territorial jurisdiction), section 1708 (theft from the mail), section 1751 (relating to Presidential assassination), section 2113 or 2114 (relating to bank and postal robbery and theft), section 2252A (relating to child pornography) where the child pornography contains a visual depiction of an actual minor engaging in sexually explicit conduct, section 2260 (production of certain child pornography for importation into the United States), section 2280 (relating to violence against maritime navigation), section 2281 (relating to violence against maritime fixed platforms), section 2319 (relating to copyright infringement), section 2320 (relating to trafficking in counterfeit goods and services), section 2332 (relating to terrorist acts abroad against United States nationals), section 2332a (relating to use of weapons of mass destruction), section 2332b (relating to international terrorist acts transcending national boundaries), section 2332g (relating to missile systems designed to destroy aircraft), section 2332h (relating to radiological dispersal devices), section 2339A or 2339B (relating to providing material support to terrorists), section 2339C (relating to financing of terrorism), or section 2339D (relating to receiving military-type training from a foreign terrorist organization) of this title, section 46502 of title 49, United States Code, a felony violation of the Chemical Diversion and Trafficking Act of 1988 (relating to precursor and essential chemicals), section 590 of the Tariff Act of 1930 (19 U.S.C. 1590) (relating to aviation smuggling), section 422 of the Controlled Substances Act (relating to transportation of drug paraphernalia), section 38(c) (relating to criminal violations) of the Arms Export Control Act, section 11 (relating to violations) of the Export Administration Act of 1979, section 206 (relating to penalties) of the International Emergency Economic Powers Act, section 16 (relating to offenses and punishment) of the Trading with the Enemy Act, any felony violation of section 15 of the Food and Nutrition Act of 2008 (relating to supplemental nutrition assistance program benefits fraud) involving a quantity of benefits having a value of not less than $5,000, any violation of section 543(a)(1) of the Housing Act of 1949 (relating to equity skimming), any felony violation of the Foreign Agents Registration Act of 1938, any felony violation of the Foreign Corrupt Practices Act, or section 92 of the Atomic Energy Act of 1954 (42 U.S.C. 2122) (relating to prohibitions governing atomic weapons) 3

environmental crimes

(E) a felony violation of the Federal Water Pollution Control Act (33 U.S.C. 1251 et seq.), the Ocean Dumping Act (33 U.S.C. 1401 et seq.), the Act to Prevent Pollution from Ships (33 U.S.C. 1901 et seq.), the Safe Drinking Water Act (42 U.S.C. 300f et seq.), or the Resources Conservation and Recovery Act (42 U.S.C. 6901 et seq.); or

(F) any act or activity constituting an offense involving a Federal health care offense;

(8) The term "State" includes a State of the United States, the District of Columbia, and any commonwealth, territory, or possession of the United States; and

(9) The term "proceeds" means any property derived from or obtained or retained, directly or indirectly, through some form of unlawful activity, including the gross receipts of such activity.

(d) Nothing in this section shall supersede any provision of Federal, State, or other law imposing criminal penalties or affording civil remedies in addition to those provided for in this section.

(e) Violations of this section may be investigated by such components of the Department of Justice as the Attorney General may direct, and by such components of the Department of the Treasury as the Secretary of the Treasury may direct, as appropriate, and, with respect to offenses over which the Department of Homeland Security has jurisdiction, by such components of the Department of Homeland Security as the Secretary of Homeland Security may direct, and, with respect to offenses over which the United States Postal Service has jurisdiction, by the Postal Service. Such authority of the Secretary of the Treasury, the Secretary of Homeland Security, and the Postal Service shall be exercised in accordance with an agreement which shall be entered into by the Secretary of the Treasury, the Secretary of Homeland Security, the Postal Service, and the Attorney General. Violations of this section involving offenses described in paragraph (c)(7)(E) may be investigated by such components of the Department of Justice as the

Attorney General may direct, and the National Enforcement Investigations Center of the Environmental Protection Agency.

(f) There is extraterritorial jurisdiction over the conduct prohibited by this section if—

(1) The conduct is by a United States citizen or, in the case of a non-United States citizen, the conduct occurs in part in the United States; and

(2) The transaction or series of related transactions involves funds or monetary instruments of a value exceeding $10,000

(g) Notice of Conviction of Financial Institutions—If any financial institution or any officer, director, or employee of any financial institution has been found guilty of an offense under this section, section 1957 or 1960 of this title, or section 5322 or 5324 of title 31, the Attorney General shall provide written notice of such fact to the appropriate regulatory agency for the financial institution.

(h) Any person who conspires to commit any offense defined in this section or section 1957 shall be subject to the same penalties as those prescribed for the offense the commission of which was the object of the conspiracy

(i) Venue—(1) Except as provided in paragraph (2), a prosecution for an offense under this section or section 1957 may be brought in—

(A) any district in which the financial or monetary transaction is conducted; or

(B) any district where a prosecution for the underlying specified unlawful activity could be brought, if the defendant participated in the transfer of the proceeds of the specified unlawful activity from that district to the district where the financial or monetary transaction is conducted.

(2) A prosecution for an attempt or conspiracy offense under this section or section 1957 may be brought in the district where venue would lie for the completed offense under paragraph (1), or in any other district where an act in furtherance of the attempt or conspiracy took place.

(3) For purposes of this section, a transfer of funds from 1 place to another, by wire or any other means, shall constitute a single, continuing transaction. Any person who conducts (as that term is defined in subsection (c)(2)) any portion of the transaction may be charged in any district in which the transaction takes place (Figure A.1).

RUNIC / CELTIC WRITING

N L R

Figure A.1 This figure represents examples of various tattoos from the NLR Gang. Gang members use tattoos to identify themselves to fellow gang members as well as rival gangs. When arrested, these tattoos are always photographed for identification purposes. As you can see in the images, members for the NLR gang tattoos vary in nature, from the location of the tattoo to its design and size.

(Continued)

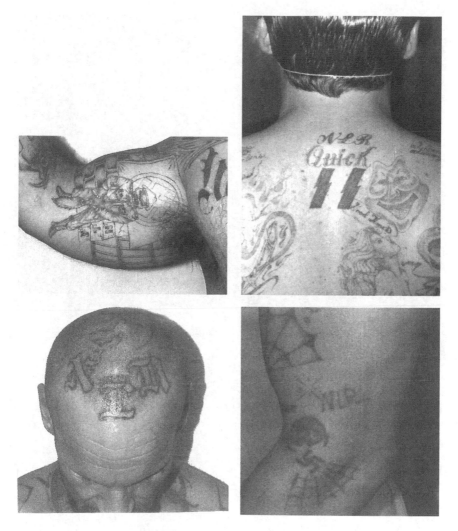

Figure A.1 (Continued) This figure represents examples of various tattoos from the NLR Gang. *(Continued)*

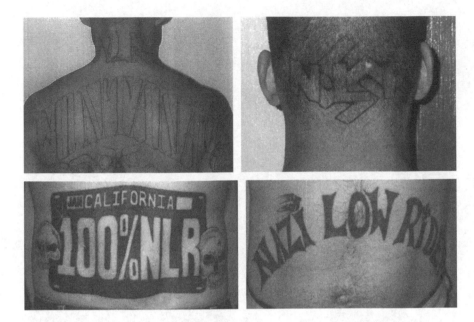

Figure A.1 (Continued)   This figure represents examples of various tattoos from the NLR Gang.

INDEX

Note: Page numbers followed by f and t refer to figures and tables, respectively.